JORDAN A. PRESTON

The 5 Trust Keys

Unlocking Deep Connection and Lasting Relationships

Copyright © 2024 by Jordan A. Preston

All rights reserved. No part of this publication may be reproduced, stored or transmitted in any form or by any means, electronic, mechanical, photocopying, recording, scanning, or otherwise without written permission from the publisher. It is illegal to copy this book, post it to a website, or distribute it by any other means without permission.

Jordan A. Preston asserts the moral right to be identified as the author of this work.

Jordan A. Preston has no responsibility for the persistence or accuracy of URLs for external or third-party Internet Websites referred to in this publication and does not guarantee that any content on such Websites is, or will remain, accurate or appropriate.

Designations used by companies to distinguish their products are often claimed as trademarks. All brand names and product names used in this book and on its cover are trade names, service marks, trademarks and registered trademarks of their respective owners. The publishers and the book are not associated with any product or vendor mentioned in this book. None of the companies referenced within the book have endorsed the book.

First edition

This book was professionally typeset on Reedsy.
Find out more at reedsy.com

To my loving parents,

Justin and Félicité,

for your unwavering support, guidance, and the countless lessons you've taught me about trust, connection, and the strength of relationships.

Your love has been my greatest inspiration.

Contents

Introduction

Why Trust Matters More Than Love?

· *Understanding the link between trust and lasting relationships*
· *Why trust is the glue that holds connections together*
· *The emotional and practical benefits of mastering trust*

When people think about relationships—whether romantic, familial, or friendships—they often focus on love. Love is the glue that holds everything together, right? But there is something even more fundamental that underpins love itself: trust.

Trust is the bedrock upon which every meaningful relationship is built. Without trust, love has no foundation, no place to grow, no soil to take root. We have all experienced moments where love was present but trust was not— times where we felt love in our hearts but couldn't share it openly because the trust had been broken or had never been established. In these moments, we learn a hard truth: **trust, not love, is the glue that binds relationships together over the long term**.

In romantic relationships, trust allows you to be vulnerable with your partner, to share your deepest thoughts, hopes, and fears without fear of betrayal or rejection. Trust fosters openness, forgiveness, and loyalty within family dynamics. In friendships, trust creates a space where mutual support can thrive. Even in professional settings, trust between colleagues fosters collaboration and teamwork.

But here's the problem: trust is often fragile, easily broken, and hard to repair. Many people don't fully understand how to build trust or what to do when it's lost. That's where this book comes in. I'm going to show you the five essential keys to building and maintaining trust in any relationship.

The Fragility of Trust

Trust is a delicate thing. It can take years to build and moments to break. A single lie, a broken promise, or an act of betrayal can shatter trust in an instant, and rebuilding it can feel like an impossible task. Therefore, so many relationships fall apart—not because the love isn't there, but because trust has been damaged beyond repair.

We live in a world where trust is constantly being tested. We've all experienced situations where someone has let us down, and the pain of that experience lingers long after the event has passed. The truth is, we all crave trust, but many of us don't know how to nurture it in our relationships.

Understanding how to build and protect trust is crucial for anyone who wants to experience deep, lasting connections with others. Whether you're trying to strengthen your marriage, heal a friendship, or create a more open and supportive family dynamic, mastering trust is the key.

Why Trust is More Important Than Ever

In today's world, the importance of trust cannot be overstated. Social media, constant connectivity, and the rapid pace of modern life have created an environment where trust is harder to establish and maintain. People are more suspicious, more guarded, and more wary of each other than ever before. Trust in institutions, the media, and even personal relationships is at an all-time low.

Amid this backdrop, the need for trust within our personal relationships has never been greater. We need to feel like we can rely on the people closest to us—our partners, family members, friends, and colleagues. We need to know that we can be vulnerable without being judged, that we can count on others to keep their promises, and that we can trust those we love to respect us, communicate openly, and take accountability when things go wrong.

The 5 Trust Keys: A Simple, Universal Framework

The *5 Trust Keys* is a framework designed to help you build, maintain, and, if necessary, restore trust in your relationships. These keys are:

1. **Vulnerability as Strength**: Learning to be open and honest, even when it's uncomfortable, is a powerful way to build trust.
2. **Consistency Over Time**: Small, consistent actions build trust over time—trust is earned, not given.
3. **Honest Communication**: Trust grows in environments where transparency and truth are the foundations of conversation.
4. **Mutual Respect**: Showing respect is essential for maintaining trust, and a lack of respect is one of the fastest ways to erode it.
5. **Shared Accountability**: Trust is a two-way street. Both parties need to take responsibility for their actions and contribute to the health of the relationship.

Each of these keys is crucial in its own right, but together they form a comprehensive approach to creating deep, meaningful connections in your life. Whether you're in a romantic relationship, working on family dynamics, or developing trust in a professional setting, these principles apply.

In the chapters ahead, we'll dive deep into each of the five trust keys, breaking down why they're essential and, more importantly, how to implement them in your life. Along the way, you'll find exercises, real-life examples, and actionable steps you can take to start building and strengthening trust immediately.

I encourage you to approach this book with an open mind and a willingness to look closely at your own relationships. You'll discover that trust isn't just something that happens to you—it's something you can actively cultivate. It's a practice, and like any practice, it gets easier and more natural the more you do it.

By the end of this journey, you'll not only have the tools to build trust with others, but you'll also find yourself feeling more confident in your ability to trust yourself. After all, self-trust is the foundation of all other relationships. Let's unlock the doors to deep, meaningful, and lasting connections.

I

Part 1: The Trust Framework

1

Chapter 1: The Fragility of Trust

- *What trust really means in relationships*
- *How trust is built and why it's often broken?*
- *The psychological and emotional cost of broken trust*

Trust is like glass. It can be beautiful, transparent, and seemingly solid, but with just one blow, it can shatter into a thousand pieces. Once broken, trust is difficult—and sometimes impossible—to restore to its original form. This chapter is about understanding the fragility of trust, why it breaks, and why it's so essential to relationships of all kinds.

What is Trust?

Trust is often described as a firm belief in the reliability, truth, or ability of someone. But in the context of relationships, it goes much deeper than that. Trust is the feeling that you can be vulnerable with someone and know that they will not take advantage of your vulnerability. It is the foundation of emotional safety in any relationship.

When we trust someone, we believe they will act in our best interest, even when we are not looking. We believe they are honest with us, that they will keep their promises, and that they will be consistent in their actions and words. Trust allows us to relax into our relationships, knowing that we are safe, respected, and valued.

However, trust is not something that is given freely. It is earned over time through actions, words, and consistency. And it can be lost in an instant.

How is Trust Built?

Trust is built incrementally, often without us even realizing it. Every time someone follows through on a promise, listens to us without judgment, or shows up when they say they will, a small piece of trust is built. These small moments accumulate over time, creating a sense of reliability and security.

The key to building trust is **consistency**. It's not one grand gesture or a single act of honesty that builds trust; it's the accumulation of many small, consistent actions over time. This is why relationships that have stood the test of time tend to have higher levels of trust—there has been enough consistency over a long period to establish a solid foundation.

Another crucial element in building trust is **vulnerability**. Trust requires a willingness to be open, to share our thoughts, fears, and desires with another person. This openness creates a bond of intimacy, where both people feel seen and understood. When we are vulnerable and our partner responds with care and understanding, trust deepens.

Why is Trust Fragile?

Despite the slow, incremental process of building trust, it can be shattered in an instant. This fragility stems from the fact that trust is fundamentally about emotional safety. When that safety is compromised—through lies, broken promises, or betrayal—the entire foundation of the relationship is shaken.

There are several key reasons trust is so fragile:

1. Trust Requires Vulnerability

At the heart of trust is vulnerability. When we trust someone, we open ourselves up to the possibility of being hurt. We share our innermost thoughts, feelings, and desires, hoping that the other person will handle them with care. When that trust is broken, the pain runs deep because it strikes at the core of our emotional safety.

2. Trust is Built Slowly, but Broken Quickly

As we've mentioned, trust takes time to build. It requires consistent, positive actions over a long period. But a single act of betrayal—whether it's infidelity, a broken promise, or dishonesty—can undo months or even years of trust-building. This is why a breach of trust can feel so devastating. The person who was once your safe harbor suddenly becomes a source of pain.

3. Trust Involves Risk

Every time we trust someone, we are taking a risk. We are putting our emotional well-being in their hands and hoping that they will not betray that trust. This risk is part of what makes trust so powerful when it is honored, but it's also what makes it so painful when it is broken. When trust is betrayed, it often feels like we've made a mistake in judgment, which can lead to feelings of shame, anger, and confusion.

The Psychological Cost of Broken Trust

The emotional and psychological cost of broken trust is significant. When trust is shattered, it can trigger a range of negative emotions—anger, sadness, betrayal, and even grief. These emotions can be overwhelming, leaving us feeling lost and unsure of how to move forward.

One of the most common reactions to broken trust is **withdrawal**. When we've been hurt, our instinct is often to protect ourselves by withdrawing from the relationship. We build emotional walls, distance ourselves from the person who hurt us, and, sometimes, shut down completely. This withdrawal is a defense mechanism—it's our way of protecting ourselves from further harm. However, it can also prevent the relationship from healing, as it creates a barrier to open communication and vulnerability.

Another common reaction is **anger**. Anger is a natural response to betrayal, but it can also be destructive if it's not managed properly. When trust is broken, anger can lead to accusations, blame, and an escalation of conflict. In some cases, this anger can be directed inward, leading to feelings of self-blame and low self-esteem.

Perhaps the most insidious effect of broken trust is the **loss of faith in future relationships**. When we've been betrayed by someone we trusted, it can be difficult to trust others in the future. We carry the wounds of past betrayals into new relationships, making it harder to be open and vulnerable. This is why some people develop trust issues after experiencing a major betrayal—they become hyper-vigilant, always on the lookout for signs that they might be hurt again.

Rebuilding Trust After it's Broken

Rebuilding trust is possible, but it's difficult. It requires time, patience, and a genuine commitment from both parties. The person who broke the trust must take full responsibility for their actions, show genuine remorse, and make consistent efforts to repair the damage. The person who was hurt must be willing to forgive, let go of resentment, and give the relationship a chance to heal.

The process of rebuilding trust often involves the following steps:

1. Acknowledgment and Apology

The first step in rebuilding trust is acknowledging the betrayal and offering a sincere apology. The person who broke the trust must take full responsibility for their actions and express genuine remorse. This apology should be more than just words—it should be accompanied by actions that demonstrate a commitment to change.

2. Open Communication

Rebuilding trust requires open, honest communication. Both parties need to be able to express their feelings, fears, and concerns without judgment or defensiveness. This may involve difficult conversations, but these conversations are necessary for healing.

3. Consistency and Follow-Through

Consistency is key when it comes to rebuilding trust. The person who broke the trust must consistently show that they are trustworthy through their actions. This means following through on promises, being reliable, and showing up for the relationship meaningfully.

4. Patience and Time

Rebuilding trust takes time. It's not something that can be rushed or forced. Both parties need to be patient and allow the healing process to unfold naturally. Trust may not be fully restored right away, but with time and consistent effort, it can be rebuilt.

5. Forgiveness

Forgiveness is an essential part of rebuilding trust. Without forgiveness, the relationship will remain stuck in a cycle of blame and resentment. Forgiveness doesn't mean forgetting or condoning the betrayal, but it does mean letting go of the anger and resentment that are holding the relationship back.

The Long-Term Effects of Trust

When trust is built and maintained, it creates a foundation for a relationship that can weather any storm. It allows for vulnerability, intimacy, and deep emotional connection. But when trust is broken, it can leave lasting scars that affect future relationships and even our ability to trust ourselves.

In the next chapters, we will explore the five trust keys that will help you build and strengthen trust in your relationships. By mastering these keys, you will be able to create a solid foundation of trust that will withstand the challenges and complexities of modern relationships.

2

Chapter 2: The Five Trust Keys

Overview of the five keys that unlock deep trust in any relationship

Key 1: Vulnerability as Strength

Key 2: Consistency Over Time

Key 3: Honest Communication

Key 4: Mutual Respect

Key 5: Shared Accountability

The balance of love and trust: Understanding the differences and overlaps

In the previous chapter, we explored the fragility of trust and why it is so essential for the foundation of any relationship. Now, we'll dive into the core of this book—the five trust keys. These are the pillars upon which deep, lasting trust is built. Understanding and applying these keys will not only help you build trust with others but also fortify your relationships in ways that create enduring bonds.

The Five Trust Keys are:

1. **Vulnerability as Strength**
2. **Consistency Over Time**
3. **Honest Communication**
4. **Mutual Respect**
5. **Shared Accountability**

Each of these keys works together to unlock a relationship built on trust. As we explore each one in detail, you'll discover practical steps you can take to implement them in your life.

Why Five Keys?

Why five? Because trust is multifaceted. It's not a simple "yes" or "no" switch, nor is it built by doing just one thing right. Trust is about actions, mindsets, and values. By understanding these five keys, you'll see how they interact and reinforce each other, creating a strong, resilient bond between people.

Let's take a closer look at each one, beginning with **Vulnerability as Strength**, the key that opens the door to authentic, deep connections.

Key 1: Vulnerability as Strength

At first glance, vulnerability might not seem like a strength. In fact, many people associate vulnerability with weakness. But in reality, vulnerability is one of the most powerful tools for building trust. When we are vulnerable, we are showing others that we trust them with our innermost thoughts, feelings, and fears. This openness invites the other person to do the same, creating a bond of trust that goes beyond surface-level interactions.

What is Vulnerability?

Vulnerability is the willingness to be open and honest about your thoughts, feelings, and experiences, even when it feels uncomfortable or risky. It's the opposite of putting up walls or wearing a mask to protect yourself.

Vulnerability means showing up as your authentic self, imperfections and all, and trusting that the other person will handle that openness with care.

In relationships, vulnerability can look like:

- Sharing your fears and insecurities with your partner.
- Admitting when you're wrong and asking for forgiveness.
- Expressing your needs and desires without fear of judgment.
- Acknowledging that you don't have all the answers and asking for help.

Why Vulnerability Builds Trust

When we are vulnerable, we are essentially saying, "I trust you enough to show you my true self." This level of openness signals to the other person that we are willing to let down our guard, which invites them to do the same. This mutual openness fosters a deeper connection and a sense of emotional safety, which is the foundation of trust.

Vulnerability also helps to break down the illusion of perfection. When we allow ourselves to be vulnerable, we show that we are human, with flaws and fears just like everyone else. This authenticity creates a space for empathy and understanding, as the other person can relate to our struggles and see us as real, relatable individuals.

Overcoming the Fear of Vulnerability

For many people, vulnerability feels terrifying. The fear of being judged, rejected, or hurt can make it difficult to open up, even in relationships where trust already exists. However, the irony is that by avoiding vulnerability, we often prevent ourselves from building the very trust we crave.

Here are a few strategies to help you embrace vulnerability:

1. **Start Small**: You don't have to share your deepest fears right away. Start with smaller, more manageable acts of vulnerability, such as admitting when you don't know something or asking for help. As you build confidence in being vulnerable, you can gradually open up more.
2. **Recognize the Rewards**: When you take the risk to be vulnerable and it is

met with empathy and understanding, you'll experience the rewards of deeper connection and trust. Remind yourself of these positive outcomes when you feel the urge to retreat into emotional walls.

3. **Practice Self-Compassion**: Vulnerability often brings up feelings of shame or inadequacy. It's important to practice self-compassion during these moments. Remind yourself that everyone experiences vulnerability and that it's a sign of strength, not weakness.

4. **Create a Safe Space**: Trust and vulnerability go hand-in-hand, so it's important to create an environment where both you and the other person feel safe to be open. This means listening without judgment, offering support, and being patient as both of you navigate moments of vulnerability.

Key 2: Consistency Over Time

Trust isn't built in a single moment; it is built over time through consistent actions. Consistency means showing up in the same reliable way, day after day, in both big and small ways. It's about keeping promises, following through on commitments, and being dependable in moments that matter.

Why Consistency is Crucial for Trust

Think about the people you trust most in your life. Chances are, they are individuals who have proven themselves to be reliable over time. They are people who do what they say they will do, who show up when you need them, and who act in a predictable and dependable manner.

Consistency builds trust because it creates a sense of reliability and stability. When we know that someone will consistently act in a certain way, we can relax into the relationship and feel safe. On the other hand, when someone is unpredictable or inconsistent, it creates anxiety and uncertainty, which can erode trust over time.

The Cumulative Power of Small Acts

One of the most powerful aspects of consistency is that it doesn't require grand gestures or major efforts. Trust is built in the small, everyday actions—keeping promises, being on time, listening when the other person speaks, and offering support in moments of need.

These small acts may seem insignificant on their own, but over time, they accumulate to create a strong foundation of trust. This is why consistency is often referred to as the "quiet builder" of trust—it's the steady, reliable actions that build trust over time, rather than the occasional grand gestures.

Building Consistency in Relationships

To build consistency in your relationships, focus on the following principles:

1. **Follow Through on Promises**: If you say you're going to do something, do it. Broken promises, even small ones, can chip away at trust.
2. **Be Predictable in a Good Way**: This doesn't mean you have to be boring or rigid, but being predictable in terms of your emotional responses and actions helps create a sense of safety. For example, if your partner knows that you will respond calmly in a stressful situation, they are more likely to trust you.
3. **Show Up, Especially in Difficult Times**: Consistency is most important during challenging moments. When things are tough, showing up for the other person—whether emotionally, physically, or mentally—builds trust in profound ways.
4. **Be Honest About What You Can and Can't Do**: Part of consistency is managing expectations. If you can't fulfill a promise or commitment, be upfront about it rather than over committing and failing to deliver. Honesty about your limitations can actually build trust.

Key 3: Honest Communication

If vulnerability is the doorway to trust, then communication is the key that opens it. Honest communication is the foundation of any trusting relationship.

It's through open, truthful conversations that we build understanding, resolve conflicts, and reinforce the trust between two people.

Why Honest Communication is Non-Negotiable

At its core, trust is about believing that the other person is being truthful with you. When we communicate honestly, we signal that we respect the other person enough to be open, even when the truth is difficult or uncomfortable. Honest communication also helps to clear up misunderstandings and prevent the buildup of resentment, which can erode trust over time.

Barriers to Honest Communication

While we all know that honesty is important, there are several barriers that can prevent us from communicating openly. These include:

- **Fear of Conflict**: Many people avoid honest communication because they fear it will lead to conflict. However, avoiding difficult conversations can create more problems in the long run.
- **Fear of Rejection or Judgment**: Sometimes, we hold back from being honest because we fear the other person's reaction. We worry that they will reject us, judge us, or be hurt by our honesty.
- **Lack of Emotional Awareness**: Honest communication requires self-awareness. If we are not in touch with our own feelings, it can be difficult to express them honestly to others.

How to Foster Honest Communication

1. **Create a Safe Space for Dialogue**: For honest communication to thrive, both parties need to feel safe to express themselves. This means listening without interrupting, offering empathy, and withholding judgment.
2. **Be Direct, But Kind**: Honesty doesn't have to be harsh. It's possible to be direct about your thoughts and feelings while still being kind and considerate of the other person's emotions.
3. **Check Your Intentions**: Before you speak, ask yourself, "Am I being

honest with the intention of building trust and understanding, or am I speaking out of anger or frustration?" Honest communication should be aimed at strengthening the relationship, not tearing the other person down.

4. **Practice Active Listening**: Honest communication is a two-way street. It's not just about expressing yourself, but also about listening to the other person with an open mind and heart.

Key 4: Mutual Respect

Respect is the cornerstone of trust. Without respect, trust cannot exist. Mutual respect means valuing the other person as an individual, honoring their feelings, boundaries, and opinions, and treating them with dignity.

Why Respect is Essential for Trust

When we respect someone, we create a space where trust can flourish. Respect signals that we see the other person as worthy of care, consideration, and honesty. Disrespect, on the other hand, undermines trust by creating an environment of belittlement, criticism, or neglect.

Respect also creates a sense of equality in the relationship. It shows that both parties are on the same level, each deserving of understanding and care. This equality fosters trust because it ensures that neither person feels superior or inferior to the other.

Cultivating Mutual Respect

1. **Honor Boundaries**: Respecting someone's boundaries—whether emotional, physical, or mental—is one of the most important ways to show respect. Trust is built when we feel that our boundaries are understood and honored.

2. **Value Their Perspective**: Even if you don't agree with the other person's opinion, it's important to respect their perspective. This means listening

without dismissing, belittling, or criticizing their viewpoint.

3. **Show Appreciation**: Regularly expressing appreciation for the other person helps to reinforce mutual respect. Acknowledge their contributions, thank them for their efforts, and recognize their value in the relationship.

4. **Avoid Disrespectful Behavior**: Criticism, sarcasm, belittling, and ignoring the other person's needs are all forms of disrespect that can quickly erode trust. Make a conscious effort to avoid these behaviors in your interactions.

Key 5: Shared Accountability

Trust is a two-way street. Both parties in a relationship must take responsibility for their actions, words, and commitments. Shared accountability means that both individuals are willing to own up to their mistakes, take responsibility for their role in conflicts, and work together to resolve issues.

Why Accountability Builds Trust

When both people in a relationship take responsibility for their actions, it creates a sense of fairness and balance. Accountability shows that each person is willing to put in the effort to make the relationship work and that they are committed to addressing issues rather than avoiding them.

Accountability also fosters trust by creating a sense of reliability. When someone takes responsibility for their actions, it signals that they are dependable and trustworthy. On the other hand, avoiding accountability—whether by blaming others or denying responsibility—undermines trust and creates resentment.

Practicing Shared Accountability

1. **Own Your Mistakes**: When you make a mistake, admit it. Taking responsibility for your actions builds trust and shows the other person that you are committed to the relationship's health.

2. **Avoid Blame**: Instead of blaming the other person when things go wrong, focus on your role in the situation. Acknowledging your part in the conflict creates a foundation for resolution and rebuilding trust.

3. **Work Together on Solutions**: Shared accountability means that both parties work together to resolve issues. This involves open communication, problem-solving, and a commitment to finding solutions that benefit both people.

4. **Follow Through on Commitments**: Accountability also means following through on your commitments, both big and small. Whether it's showing up on time, keeping a promise, or doing your part in a joint effort, consistency in accountability builds trust.

Conclusion: The Power of the 5 Trust Keys

By mastering these five trust keys—vulnerability as strength, consistency over time, honest communication, mutual respect, and shared accountability—you will be able to build trust in all areas of your life. Whether you're working on a romantic relationship, deepening your connection with family, or building trust in a professional setting, these keys are universal.

Trust is not something that happens by chance; it is something you cultivate through intentional actions, words, and behaviors. By applying these trust keys, you'll create relationships that are not only strong and lasting but also deeply fulfilling.

II

Part 2: Deepening Trust in Special Relationships

3

Chapter 3: Trust in Romantic Relationships

- *How to apply the five trust keys in romantic partnerships*
- *Building trust after betrayal*
- *The role of intimacy in strengthening trust*

Romantic relationships are perhaps the most emotionally charged and intimate of all human connections. In these relationships, trust is the cornerstone that allows vulnerability, love, and intimacy to flourish. But trust in romantic partnerships can be complex, often facing challenges unique to the emotional intensity of these bonds.

In this chapter, we'll explore how the five trust keys—vulnerability, consistency, honest communication, mutual respect, and shared accountability—can help strengthen trust in romantic relationships. We'll also address how to rebuild trust after betrayal, and the role intimacy plays in fostering deeper connections.

The Importance of Trust in Romantic Relationships

Trust is the foundation of a healthy, loving relationship. Without it, partners struggle to feel safe, valued, and emotionally connected. Trust allows couples to be vulnerable with one another, share their innermost thoughts and feelings, and feel secure in the knowledge that their partner will support and care for them.

When trust is strong, couples can navigate life's inevitable ups and downs with resilience and grace. They know they can rely on each other in times of crisis, and they feel confident in the stability of their relationship. Conversely, when trust is weak or broken, the entire relationship can become strained. Insecurity, jealousy, and conflict often take root, eroding the emotional connection between partners.

In romantic relationships, trust is not just about fidelity or loyalty, though those are certainly important aspects. Trust also means knowing that your partner will:

- **Keep their promises and commitments**
- **Support you during difficult times**
- **Respect your boundaries**
- **Communicate openly and honestly**
- **Treat you with kindness and care**

Building and maintaining this kind of trust requires intentional effort, consistent behavior, and a willingness to be open and vulnerable with each other. Let's explore how each of the five trust keys can be applied in romantic relationships.

Key 1: Vulnerability as Strength in Romantic Relationships

Vulnerability in romantic relationships is about more than just sharing your emotions—it's about showing your partner who you truly are, flaws and all. It's about being brave enough to let your guard down, knowing that your partner will not use your vulnerabilities against you.

In the early stages of a relationship, vulnerability might involve sharing your past experiences, hopes, and fears. As the relationship deepens, vulnerability can mean discussing difficult topics, like past hurts or insecurities, without fear of judgment.

Why Vulnerability Builds Intimacy

In romantic relationships, vulnerability fosters intimacy by creating a space for deeper emotional connection. When both partners feel safe enough to be vulnerable, they can share parts of themselves that they may keep hidden from the rest of the world. This emotional transparency allows couples to understand each other on a deeper level, which strengthens the bond between them.

When we are vulnerable, we invite our partner to see us in our most authentic form. This can be scary, but it's also what creates real intimacy. Without vulnerability, relationships remain superficial, lacking the depth needed to sustain trust over time.

Overcoming Fear of Vulnerability in Romantic Relationships

It's common to fear being vulnerable with a romantic partner, especially if you've been hurt in the past. However, vulnerability is essential for building trust and intimacy. Here are some tips for embracing vulnerability in your relationship:

1. **Start with Small Steps**: Begin by sharing small, personal details that you may not have revealed yet. As your comfort grows, you can gradually open up about deeper topics.

2. **Acknowledge the Fear**: It's okay to admit to your partner that being vulnerable feels scary. By acknowledging this fear, you create an opportunity for your partner to support you in overcoming it.

3. **Create a Safe Environment**: Make sure that both you and your partner feel safe to be vulnerable. This means practicing empathy, listening without judgment, and offering reassurance when needed.

4. **Accept Imperfections**: Remember that no one is perfect, and vulnerability involves embracing your imperfections. Trust that your partner will appreciate your authenticity.

Key 2: Consistency Over Time in Romantic Relationships

In romantic relationships, consistency is essential for building and maintaining trust. Consistency doesn't just mean being reliable in the big moments; it's about showing up day after day in small, meaningful ways. This could be as simple as checking in with your partner about their day, being there when you say you will, or following through on promises, no matter how small.

The Power of Small Acts in Building Trust

In relationships, it's often the little things that matter most. Remembering your partner's favorite snack, sending a good morning text, or being there to listen at the end of a tough day—these small acts of consistency build trust over time. Each one reinforces the message, "I am here for you, and you can count on me."

On the other hand, inconsistency can create uncertainty and insecurity. When a partner is unpredictable—saying one thing and doing another—it can erode trust and lead to feelings of doubt or mistrust. For example, if one partner promises to spend more quality time together but frequently cancels plans, it sends the message that they are not reliable.

Building Consistency in Your Relationship

To build trust through consistency, focus on the following strategies:

1. **Follow Through on Commitments**: If you tell your partner you will do something—whether it's a small task or a major promise—make sure you follow through. Consistently keeping your word builds trust over time.

2. **Be Emotionally Consistent**: Emotional consistency means responding to your partner's needs and feelings in a stable, predictable way. For example, if your partner shares something vulnerable, respond with compassion and understanding, rather than unpredictability.

3. **Communicate When You Can't Deliver**: Sometimes, life gets in the way, and we can't always meet every commitment. In those cases, communicate openly with your partner and explain why you're unable to follow through. Being transparent can help preserve trust even when

plans change.

Key 3: Honest Communication in Romantic Relationships

Honest communication is the lifeblood of trust in any relationship, but it is especially important in romantic partnerships. Without honest communication, misunderstandings, assumptions, and unspoken resentments can fester, leading to conflict and a breakdown of trust.

Why Honest Communication is Crucial for Trust

When couples communicate openly and honestly, they create an environment where both partners feel understood, valued, and heard. Honest communication also helps to clarify expectations, resolve conflicts, and prevent the buildup of resentment. In romantic relationships, being honest means not only sharing your feelings and concerns but also being transparent about your intentions, needs, and boundaries.

Navigating Difficult Conversations

One of the most challenging aspects of honest communication is addressing difficult topics, such as disagreements, unmet needs, or past hurts. Many couples avoid these conversations because they fear they will lead to conflict or hurt feelings. However, avoiding difficult conversations can actually harm the relationship in the long run.

Here's how to approach honest communication, even when it's tough:

1. **Use "I" Statements**: When expressing your feelings, focus on how you feel, rather than placing blame on your partner. For example, instead of saying, "You never listen to me," try saying, "I feel unheard when I don't get a chance to share my thoughts."

2. **Practice Active Listening**: Honest communication isn't just about talking—it's about listening. Make sure to give your partner your full attention when they are speaking, and listen with the intent to understand, not just to respond.

3. **Be Open to Feedback**: Part of being honest is being open to hearing your

partner's perspective, even if it's not easy to hear. Accept feedback with an open mind and a willingness to improve.

Key 4: Mutual Respect in Romantic Relationships

Respect is essential for maintaining trust in any romantic relationship. When we respect our partner, we show that we value them as a person and honor their needs, boundaries, and individuality. Mutual respect fosters a sense of equality and balance in the relationship, which is necessary for building lasting trust.

How Respect Reinforces Trust

Respect and trust go hand in hand. When couples treat each other with respect, they create a safe environment where both partners feel valued and heard. Disrespect, on the other hand, can quickly erode trust. Criticism, belittling, and dismissing your partner's feelings or opinions can lead to resentment and a breakdown of trust.

Ways to Show Respect in Romantic Relationships

1. **Honor Boundaries**: Respecting your partner's boundaries—whether emotional, physical, or mental—is crucial for maintaining trust. Make sure you are aware of your partner's boundaries and make an effort to honor them.

2. **Value Your Partner's Perspective**: Even if you don't agree with your partner's viewpoint, it's important to respect their perspective. Show them that you value their opinion by listening without interrupting or dismissing their thoughts.

3. **Express Appreciation**: Regularly expressing gratitude and appreciation for your partner reinforces mutual respect. Take time to acknowledge the things your partner does for you and let them know how much you value their contributions to the relationship.

Key 5: Shared Accountability in Romantic Relationships

In romantic relationships, accountability is about taking responsibility for your actions and words. When both partners are willing to own up to their mistakes and work together to resolve conflicts, trust is reinforced. On the other hand, avoiding accountability—whether by blaming your partner, denying responsibility, or making excuses—can quickly erode trust.

The Importance of Accountability in Romantic Relationships

Accountability fosters trust by showing that both partners are committed to the health of the relationship. It demonstrates that each person is willing to take responsibility for their role in conflicts and make amends when necessary. Shared accountability also helps to create a sense of balance in the relationship, as both partners take equal responsibility for maintaining trust and resolving issues.

Practicing Shared Accountability

1. **Own Your Mistakes**: When you make a mistake, be willing to admit it. Taking responsibility for your actions builds trust and shows your partner that you are committed to the relationship's growth.
2. **Avoid Blame**: Blaming your partner for problems in the relationship can create defensiveness and erode trust. Instead of pointing fingers, focus on how you can both work together to resolve the issue.
3. **Follow Through on Commitments**: Accountability also means following through on your promises and commitments, both big and small. Consistently keeping your word builds trust over time.

Rebuilding Trust After Betrayal

Betrayal in a romantic relationship—whether it's infidelity, dishonesty, or another form of broken trust—can feel devastating. However, rebuilding trust after betrayal is possible with time, commitment, and a willingness from both partners to heal.

Steps to Rebuild Trust

1. **Acknowledge the Betrayal**: The first step in rebuilding trust is acknowledging the betrayal and its impact on the relationship. Both partners need to openly discuss what happened and how it affected their trust in each other.

2. **Offer a Sincere Apology**: The person who broke the trust must offer a genuine apology and take full responsibility for their actions. This apology should be accompanied by efforts to rebuild trust through consistent behavior and accountability.

3. **Create a Plan for Moving Forward**: Rebuilding trust requires a plan for how both partners will work to restore the relationship. This may include open communication, setting boundaries, and seeking professional help if needed.

4. **Be Patient**: Rebuilding trust takes time. Both partners need to be patient and allow the healing process to unfold naturally. Trust may not be fully restored immediately, but with consistent effort, it can be rebuilt.

The Role of Intimacy in Strengthening Trust

Intimacy and trust are deeply intertwined. As trust grows, so does the ability to be emotionally and physically intimate with your partner. Intimacy allows couples to connect on a deeper level, reinforcing the bond of trust between them.

Fostering Emotional and Physical Intimacy

1. **Create Emotional Intimacy**: Emotional intimacy involves sharing your innermost thoughts, feelings, and desires with your partner. It's about being vulnerable and allowing your partner to see the real you.

2. **Nurture Physical Intimacy**: Physical intimacy is an important aspect of romantic relationships. It's not just about sex—it's also about physical affection, like holding hands, hugging, and cuddling, which reinforce feelings of closeness and trust.

Conclusion: Trust is the Foundation of Love

Trust is the foundation of love in any romantic relationship. Without trust, love cannot fully flourish, and without love, trust may feel empty. By applying the *five trust keys*—**vulnerability, consistency, honest communication, mutual respect, and shared accountability**—you can build a relationship that is not only loving but also deeply trusting.

As we move into the next chapter, we'll explore how to apply these same principles in family dynamics, where trust can often be complicated by history, generational differences, and unresolved conflicts.

4

Chapter 4: Trust in Family Dynamics

- *Trust-building strategies for parents, siblings, and children*
- *Breaking generational cycles of mistrust*

Family relationships are unique. Unlike romantic or friendship bonds, we don't choose our family members. We are born into these relationships, and they often span our entire lives. Trust within a family is foundational for creating a supportive and nurturing environment, but it is often more complicated than in other relationships. Family dynamics are influenced by years of shared history, familial expectations, generational values, and cultural traditions, all of which can make trust more challenging to navigate.

In this chapter, we'll explore how to apply the five trust keys to strengthen trust in family relationships—whether between parents and children, siblings, or extended family members. We'll also discuss how to break cycles of mistrust that often persist across generations and how to rebuild trust when family bonds have been strained.

The Importance of Trust in Family Relationships

Trust is the cornerstone of any healthy family dynamic. When family members trust one another, they create a safe and supportive environment where everyone feels valued, respected, and heard. This sense of security fosters deeper emotional connections and encourages open communication, making it easier to navigate the challenges and conflicts that inevitably arise in families.

Without trust, family relationships can become strained or dysfunctional. Mistrust often leads to secrecy, unresolved conflicts, and emotional distance, all of which undermine the sense of belonging that families are meant to provide. In families where trust has been broken—whether through dishonesty, betrayal, or neglect—it can feel nearly impossible to repair the damage, especially when the hurt has lingered for years or even decades.

Rebuilding trust within a family is a process that requires patience, consistency, and a willingness from all parties to engage in open, honest communication. Let's examine how each of the five trust keys can be applied to build and maintain trust in family relationships.

Key 1: Vulnerability as Strength in Family Dynamics

Vulnerability in family relationships is often complicated by long-standing roles and expectations. For example, parents may feel pressure to appear strong and authoritative, while children may fear being judged or misunderstood by their parents. Siblings might avoid vulnerability to protect themselves from comparisons or rivalries. Despite these challenges, vulnerability is essential for building trust within families.

Why Vulnerability is Important in Families

When family members allow themselves to be vulnerable, they open the door to deeper emotional connections. Vulnerability helps to humanize family members, allowing them to see each other as individuals with their own fears, insecurities, and desires. This shared openness fosters empathy and understanding, which are critical for building trust.

Vulnerability can also help break down entrenched family dynamics. In many families, roles are established early on and can be difficult to change. For example, one sibling may always be seen as the "responsible one," while another is labeled the "troublemaker." These roles can create barriers to vulnerability because family members may feel locked into certain expectations.

By being vulnerable, family members can break free from these roles and allow themselves to be seen in a more authentic light.

Encouraging Vulnerability in Family Relationships

1. **Lead by Example**: If you want your family members to be more vulnerable with you, start by modeling vulnerability yourself. Share your feelings, admit when you're struggling, and be open about your insecurities. This creates a safe space for others to do the same.

2. **Create a Non-Judgmental Environment**: Vulnerability can only thrive in an environment where family members feel safe from judgment or criticism. Make it clear that all feelings and experiences are valid, and offer support rather than solutions or judgments.

3. **Acknowledge Past Hurts**: Vulnerability often involves addressing past wounds or unresolved conflicts. Be willing to discuss these issues openly and with compassion, even if they are difficult to talk about.

Key 2: Consistency Over Time in Family Dynamics

Consistency is vital in family relationships because it creates a sense of reliability and security. This is especially important in parent-child relationships, where children need to feel that they can count on their parents to be there for them—both emotionally and physically. But consistency is equally important in sibling relationships, as well as extended family dynamics.

The Role of Consistency in Family Trust

Consistency means being present, reliable, and emotionally stable in your interactions with family members. It means showing up when you say you will, keeping your promises, and offering support when needed. Inconsistent behavior—such as broken promises, unpredictability, or emotional distance—can create insecurity and mistrust, particularly in children.

In families where inconsistency has been a pattern, it can take time to rebuild trust. For example, if a parent has been absent or emotionally unavailable, their children may have difficulty trusting them even after they've committed to change. In these cases, consistency over time is crucial for restoring trust.

Building Consistency in Family Relationships

1. **Keep Promises**: Whether it's attending a school event or simply following through on a commitment to spend time together, keeping promises is essential for building trust. Broken promises, especially from parents, can leave lasting scars on children.

2. **Be Emotionally Consistent**: In families, emotional consistency is just as important as physical consistency. This means responding to family members with care and stability, rather than unpredictability or volatility.

3. **Show Up, Even When It's Hard**: In families, some of the most important moments for building trust happen during difficult times. Whether it's offering support during a family crisis or being there for a sibling in need, consistently showing up strengthens family bonds.

Key 3: Honest Communication in Family Dynamics

Honest communication is often more challenging in families because of the complex dynamics at play. Family members may avoid certain topics to keep the peace, or they may struggle with unspoken expectations and assumptions. However, without honest communication, misunderstandings and resentments can build, creating emotional distance and eroding trust.

The Challenge of Honest Communication in Families

One of the biggest challenges in family communication is the tendency to avoid difficult conversations. Parents may avoid discussing sensitive topics with their children out of fear of causing conflict, while children may hide their true feelings to avoid disappointing their parents. Siblings may struggle with unresolved rivalries or comparisons, which can lead to a lack of open communication.

In families where communication has been strained, it's common for certain issues to remain unspoken for years, creating a sense of emotional distance and mistrust. Breaking this cycle requires a commitment to honest, open dialogue, even when it's uncomfortable.

Fostering Honest Communication in Families

1. **Address Unspoken Issues**: In many families, certain topics are avoided because they are seen as too painful or difficult to discuss. However, avoiding these conversations only leads to more mistrust. Be willing to address the "elephant in the room" and engage in open, honest dialogue about difficult issues.

2. **Encourage Open Dialogue Without Judgment**: Create an environment where family members feel safe to express their true feelings without fear of judgment or criticism. Encourage open dialogue, even when opinions differ.

3. **Be Transparent About Expectations**: Misunderstandings often arise in families due to unspoken expectations. Be clear about your needs and expectations, and encourage others to do the same.

Key 4: Mutual Respect in Family Dynamics

Mutual respect is essential for maintaining trust in any family relationship. Respect means honoring each family member's individuality, boundaries, and feelings. Without respect, family relationships can become fraught with conflict, resentment, and power struggles, all of which erode trust.

Why Respect is Vital in Families

Respect is particularly important in parent-child relationships, as it sets the tone for how family members interact with one another. When parents respect their children's boundaries and feelings, they model healthy, respectful behavior that children carry into their own relationships. Similarly, when siblings respect each other's differences and individuality, they create an environment where trust can flourish.

However, respect is often one of the first things to break down in families. Parents may dismiss their children's feelings or opinions, siblings may engage in rivalry or teasing, and extended family members may overstep boundaries. Restoring respect in these relationships is crucial for rebuilding trust.

Cultivating Respect in Family Relationships

1. **Respect Boundaries**: Every family member has their own emotional and physical boundaries. Whether it's respecting your child's privacy or honoring your sibling's need for space, respecting boundaries is a key part of building trust.

2. **Acknowledge Individuality**: Family members are individuals with their own thoughts, feelings, and experiences. Respect each person's individuality, even if their choices or perspectives differ from your own.

3. **Model Respectful Behavior**: As a parent or family leader, your actions set the tone for the rest of the family. Model respectful behavior by listening without interrupting, honoring commitments, and treating all family members with dignity.

Key 5: Shared Accountability in Family Dynamics

In family relationships, accountability means taking responsibility for your actions, words, and role in the family dynamic. Shared accountability fosters trust by ensuring that all family members are held to the same standard of behavior, rather than allowing certain individuals to avoid responsibility or blame others.

Why Accountability Is Essential in Families

In families where accountability is lacking, trust is often eroded by unresolved conflicts, unacknowledged mistakes, and unspoken grievances. For example, if a parent consistently blames their child for problems in the family without acknowledging their own role, it creates a power imbalance that undermines trust.

Shared accountability means that everyone in the family takes responsibility for their actions and works together to resolve conflicts. This creates a sense of fairness and trust, as each family member knows that they will not be unfairly blamed or judged.

Practicing Shared Accountability in Families

1. **Own Your Mistakes**: When you make a mistake, be willing to admit it and take responsibility for your actions. This sets a positive example for the rest of the family and helps to build trust.
2. **Avoid Blame**: Blaming others for problems in the family only creates more conflict and mistrust. Instead of pointing fingers, focus on how you can contribute to resolving the issue.
3. **Work Together to Resolve Conflicts**: Shared accountability means that all family members are involved in resolving conflicts. Whether it's addressing a misunderstanding between siblings or navigating a family crisis, working together fosters a sense of unity and trust.

Breaking Generational Cycles of Mistrust

In many families, patterns of mistrust are passed down from generation to generation. For example, a parent who was raised in an environment of secrecy and emotional distance may unintentionally replicate these behaviors with their own children. Breaking these cycles requires conscious effort and a commitment to creating a new dynamic based on trust, openness, and respect.

Steps to Break Generational Patterns of Mistrust

1. **Recognize the Pattern**: The first step in breaking a generational cycle of mistrust is recognizing it. Take time to reflect on the patterns of behavior that have been passed down in your family and how they may be affecting your current relationships.
2. **Commit to Change**: Breaking a generational cycle requires a conscious commitment to change. This may involve adopting new communication strategies, setting healthier boundaries, or seeking professional help to address deep-rooted issues.
3. **Lead by Example**: As a parent or family leader, your actions have a powerful influence on the rest of the family. By modeling trust-building behaviors, you can help to shift the family dynamic and create a new

legacy of trust.

Conclusion: Trust as the Foundation of Family Bonds

Trust is the foundation of all healthy family relationships. By applying the five trust keys—vulnerability, consistency, honest communication, mutual respect, and shared accountability—you can strengthen trust within your family and create a more supportive, nurturing environment. Whether you are building trust with your children, siblings, or extended family members, these principles will help you navigate the complexities of family dynamics and foster deeper, more meaningful connections.

In the next chapter, we'll explore how to apply these same principles in friendships and professional relationships, where trust is equally important but often more nuanced.

5

Chapter 5: Trust in Friendships and at Work

- *How to use trust keys in platonic relationships and professional settings*
- *Trust as the basis for long-lasting friendships*
- *Trust at work: Building strong team dynamics*

In both our personal and professional lives, trust is the cornerstone of meaningful and productive relationships. Friendships enrich our lives with support, joy, and companionship, while professional relationships influence our careers, collaboration, and daily satisfaction. Trust empowers these relationships to thrive, fostering environments where individuals feel valued, respected, and connected.

In this chapter, we'll delve into how the five trust keys—**vulnerability, consistency**, **honest communication**, **mutual respect**, and **shared accountability**—apply specifically to friendships and professional relationships. We'll explore practical strategies to build, maintain, and, when necessary, repair trust in these vital areas of our lives.

Trust in Friendships

Friendships are unique bonds formed through mutual affection, shared experiences, and common interests. Unlike family relationships, we choose our friends, and these relationships often reflect our values and personalities. Trust in friendships allows us to share our true selves without fear of judgment or betrayal, deepening the connection and enhancing the quality of our lives.

Key 1: Vulnerability as Strength in Friendships

Vulnerability in friendships means sharing personal thoughts, feelings, and experiences openly. It involves taking emotional risks by expressing fears, dreams, and insecurities.

Why Vulnerability Matters

- **Deepens Connection**: Sharing vulnerabilities fosters intimacy and understanding.
- **Builds Empathy**: Friends can offer support when they understand your experiences.
- **Encourages Reciprocity**: Your openness invites others to share, strengthening mutual trust.

Practicing Vulnerability

1. **Share Personal Stories**: Discuss experiences that have shaped you.
2. **Express Emotions Freely**: Be honest about how you feel, both positive and negative.
3. **Seek Support When Needed**: Reach out during tough times instead of isolating yourself.

Creating a Safe Space

- **Active Listening**: Give full attention without interrupting.
- **Non-Judgmental Attitude**: Accept your friend's feelings without criticism.
- **Confidentiality**: Respect the privacy of shared information.

Key 2: Consistency Over Time in Friendships

Consistency establishes reliability. Friends who are dependable reinforce trust through their actions.

Building Consistency

1. **Keep Commitments**: Honor plans and promises.
2. **Be Present**: Regularly check in, showing you value the relationship.
3. **Support Through Challenges**: Stand by your friends during difficult times.

The Impact of Inconsistency

- **Erodes Trust**: Unreliable behavior creates doubt.
- **Creates Distance**: Friends may withdraw if they feel they can't rely on you.

Key 3: Honest Communication in Friendships

Open and honest communication prevents misunderstandings and resolves conflicts.

Practicing Honest Communication

1. **Express Needs and Boundaries**: Clearly articulate your expectations.
2. **Provide Constructive Feedback**: Offer insights with kindness and respect.
3. **Address Issues Promptly**: Tackle problems before they escalate.

Navigating Difficult Conversations

- **Use "I" Statements**: Focus on your feelings to avoid blame.
- **Choose the Right Moment**: Find a time when both parties are calm.

- **Listen Actively**: Understand your friend's perspective fully.

Key 4: Mutual Respect in Friendships

Respect involves valuing each other's individuality, opinions, and boundaries.

Demonstrating Respect

1. **Honor Differences**: Appreciate diverse viewpoints and backgrounds.
2. **Respect Boundaries**: Acknowledge personal limits regarding time, topics, and space.
3. **Show Appreciation**: Express gratitude for the friendship.

The Role of Respect in Trust

- **Fosters Safety**: Friends feel secure to be themselves.
- **Enhances Communication**: Open dialogue thrives in respectful environments.

Key 5: Shared Accountability in Friendships

Shared accountability means both friends take responsibility for their actions and contributions to the relationship.

Practicing Shared Accountability

1. **Own Mistakes**: Admit when you're wrong and apologize sincerely.
2. **Avoid Blame Game**: Focus on solutions rather than fault.
3. **Collaborate on Solutions**: Work together to overcome challenges.

Trust in Professional Relationships

In the workplace, trust is essential for effective collaboration, innovation, and a positive organizational culture. Professional relationships built on trust lead to increased productivity, job satisfaction, and overall success.

Key 1: Vulnerability as Strength in Professional Settings

While vulnerability in the workplace must be balanced with professionalism, appropriate openness can build stronger teams.

Why Vulnerability Matters at Work

- **Enhances Collaboration**: Openness encourages idea sharing.
- **Builds Team Cohesion**: Understanding colleagues fosters empathy.
- **Promotes Learning**: Admitting knowledge gaps allows for growth.

Practicing Appropriate Vulnerability

1. **Admit Mistakes**: Acknowledge errors to build credibility.
2. **Seek Feedback**: Show willingness to improve.
3. **Share Insights**: Offer personal experiences that can benefit the team.

Key 2: Consistency Over Time in Professional Relationships

Reliability is crucial in professional settings. Consistent performance and behavior build trust among colleagues and superiors.

Building Consistency

1. **Meet Deadlines**: Deliver work on time.
2. **Maintain Quality**: Provide consistent, high-quality output.
3. **Communicate Regularly**: Keep stakeholders informed.

Effects of Inconsistency

- **Damages Reputation**: Unreliability can hinder career progression.
- **Affects Team Performance**: Others may be impacted by inconsistent contributions.

Key 3: Honest Communication in Professional Relationships

Transparent communication promotes efficiency and prevents misunderstandings.

Practicing Honest Communication

1. **Provide Clear Updates**: Keep others informed about progress and challenges.
2. **Offer Constructive Feedback**: Help colleagues improve with respectful suggestions.
3. **Address Conflicts Directly**: Resolve issues professionally and promptly.

Effective Communication Strategies

- **Be Solution-Oriented**: Focus on resolving issues.
- **Maintain Professionalism**: Keep emotions in check during discussions.
- **Respect Hierarchies**: Communicate appropriately within organizational structures.

Key 4: Mutual Respect in Professional Relationships

Respect in the workplace creates a positive environment where everyone feels valued.

Demonstrating Respect

1. **Acknowledge Expertise**: Recognize and appreciate others' skills.

2. **Embrace Diversity**: Respect different backgrounds and perspectives.
3. **Practice Courtesy**: Use polite language and manners.

Benefits of Mutual Respect

- **Enhances Teamwork**: Respectful environments encourage collaboration.
- **Reduces Conflict**: Mutual respect minimizes misunderstandings.

Key 5: Shared Accountability in Professional Relationships

Accountability ensures that everyone contributes fairly and takes responsibility for their work.

Practicing Shared Accountability

1. **Set Clear Expectations**: Define roles and responsibilities.
2. **Monitor Progress**: Regularly review tasks and deadlines.
3. **Address Issues Collectively**: Work together to solve problems.

Promoting a Culture of Accountability

- **Lead by Example**: Model accountable behavior.
- **Encourage Ownership**: Empower others to take charge of their tasks.
- **Provide Support**: Offer assistance when colleagues face challenges.

Building Trust Across Cultures and Teams

In today's globalized world, we often interact with people from diverse backgrounds. Cultural differences can influence perceptions of trust.

Understanding Cultural Impacts on Trust

- **Communication Styles**: Direct vs. indirect communication can affect understanding.

- **Power Distance**: Attitudes toward authority vary across cultures.
- **Individualism vs. Collectivism**: Preferences for teamwork or independent work differ.

Strategies for Building Trust in Diverse Settings

1. **Cultural Awareness**: Educate yourself about different cultural norms.
2. **Adaptability**: Be flexible in your communication and behavior.
3. **Inclusive Practices**: Create environments where everyone feels welcome.

Repairing Trust in Friendships and Work

Despite best efforts, trust can sometimes be broken. Repairing it requires effort from all parties involved.

Steps to Rebuild Trust

1. **Acknowledge the Breach**: Recognize and admit the issue.
2. **Offer a Genuine Apology**: Express remorse sincerely.
3. **Make Amends**: Take actions to rectify the situation.
4. **Establish New Agreements**: Set clear expectations moving forward.
5. **Be Patient**: Understand that rebuilding trust takes time.

Maintaining Trust Over Time

Trust is not a one-time achievement but an ongoing practice.

Tips for Sustaining Trust

- **Continuous Communication**: Keep lines of dialogue open.
- **Regular Reflection**: Assess the health of your relationships periodically.
- **Adapt to Changes**: Be willing to evolve as circumstances shift.

Conclusion

Trust in friendships and professional relationships enriches our lives and contributes to personal and collective success. By applying the five trust keys thoughtfully and consistently, we can build stronger, more fulfilling connections that stand the test of time.

III

Part 3: Repairing Broken Trust

6

Chapter 6: Healing After Betrayal

- *How to repair trust after infidelity or other serious breaches*
- *The role of forgiveness in rebuilding trust*
- *Practical steps for restoring broken connections*

Betrayal is one of the most devastating experiences in any relationship, whether it occurs in romantic partnerships, friendships, family, or professional settings. Trust, as we've discussed, is the foundation of any healthy relationship, and betrayal is the ultimate violation of that trust. When betrayal happens—whether through infidelity, dishonesty, broken promises, or deceit—the emotional impact can be profound, often leaving a trail of pain, anger, and loss.

However, while betrayal is deeply painful, healing is possible. Rebuilding trust after betrayal is a complex and delicate process, but with time, effort, and commitment, it can lead to a renewed and even stronger relationship. In this chapter, we'll explore the steps to healing after betrayal, how to rebuild trust, and how to move forward with greater understanding and emotional resilience.

The Emotional Impact of Betrayal

Betrayal strikes at the core of trust, often triggering a range of intense emotions. These emotions are not only painful but also disorienting, leaving the betrayed person questioning everything they thought they knew about the relationship.

Common Emotional Responses to Betrayal

1. **Shock and Disbelief**: Many people are initially in shock after a betrayal. They may struggle to comprehend that the person they trusted could hurt them in such a significant way. This disbelief can make the situation feel surreal, as if it's happening to someone else.

2. **Anger and Resentment**: Anger is a common response to betrayal. The person who has been hurt may feel enraged at the betrayal itself, at the person who betrayed them, or even at themselves for not seeing the signs earlier. Resentment can build, especially if the betrayal has gone on for a long time or has caused significant damage.

3. **Hurt and Sadness**: Beneath the anger, there is often deep emotional pain. Betrayal cuts deeply because it involves a violation of trust, which is central to any meaningful connection. The pain of betrayal can feel like a personal rejection or abandonment, leading to intense sadness and grief.

4. **Fear and Insecurity**: Betrayal shakes the foundation of security in a relationship. It can lead to feelings of insecurity, not only about the future of the relationship but also about the self. Many people experience fear that they will be hurt again or that they can no longer trust their judgment in relationships.

5. **Self-Doubt and Shame**: Betrayal can lead to self-doubt, with the person wondering if they did something wrong or if they were somehow at fault for the betrayal. They may also feel shame for not recognizing the betrayal earlier or for staying in the relationship despite the warning signs.

6. **Loss of Trust in Others**: After experiencing betrayal, many people find it difficult to trust others, not just the person who betrayed them. The pain of betrayal can create a general mistrust of people, making it challenging to form new relationships or trust old ones.

Steps to Healing After Betrayal

Healing after betrayal is a process that requires time, patience, and a commitment to personal and relational growth. It involves not only repairing the relationship, if that is the goal, but also healing emotionally as an individual.

1. Acknowledge the Betrayal and Its Impact

The first step in healing is acknowledging the betrayal and the emotions that come with it. This means being honest with yourself about the extent of the betrayal and allowing yourself to feel the full range of emotions, no matter how painful they may be.

- **Accept Your Feelings**: Allow yourself to feel angry, hurt, sad, or betrayed. Trying to suppress or ignore these emotions will only prolong the healing process. Acknowledging your feelings is the first step toward processing them and eventually moving forward.
- **Avoid Rushing the Process**: Healing after betrayal takes time. Don't pressure yourself to "get over it" too quickly. Give yourself the space to grieve the loss of trust and process the emotional fallout of the betrayal.

2. Confront the Betrayal Openly

Once you've acknowledged the betrayal internally, the next step is to confront the person who betrayed you. This conversation is often difficult, but it is necessary for healing to begin.

- **Communicate Honestly**: Express how the betrayal has affected you, both emotionally and in terms of the relationship. Use "I" statements to focus on your feelings and experience, such as "I feel hurt and betrayed because of what happened."
- **Listen to Their Response**: While you may be focused on your own hurt, it's important to listen to the other person's side of the story. They may offer an explanation, an apology, or an acknowledgment of their actions. However, be prepared for the possibility that they may not take full responsibility, which can complicate the healing process.

- **Set Boundaries for the Conversation**: Make it clear that this conversation is about addressing the betrayal, not about shifting blame or engaging in further conflict. If emotions become too heated, take a break and revisit the conversation when both parties are calmer.

3. Decide on the Future of the Relationship

After confronting the betrayal, you must decide whether you want to continue the relationship or end it. This decision depends on several factors, including the severity of the betrayal, the willingness of both parties to work on repairing the relationship, and your own emotional needs.

- **Assess the Possibility of Forgiveness**: Forgiveness is not about excusing the betrayal but about letting go of the anger and resentment that can keep you stuck in the past. Consider whether you are able to eventually forgive the other person, or if the betrayal has caused irreparable damage to your trust.
- **Evaluate the Other Person's Commitment**: Rebuilding trust after betrayal requires a genuine commitment from the person who betrayed you. Are they willing to take responsibility for their actions? Are they committed to making changes and doing the work to regain your trust? Without this commitment, it may be difficult to move forward.
- **Consider Your Own Emotional Health**: Ultimately, the decision to continue or end the relationship should be based on what is healthiest for you. If the betrayal has caused too much pain or if the other person is unwilling to change, it may be in your best interest to let go and move on.

4. Begin the Process of Forgiveness

If you decide to continue the relationship, forgiveness becomes an essential part of the healing process. Forgiveness is not a one-time event but a gradual process that unfolds over time. It involves letting go of the desire for revenge or punishment and choosing to release the resentment that has built up from the betrayal.

- **Understanding Forgiveness**: Forgiveness does not mean forgetting what happened or pretending that the betrayal didn't hurt. It also doesn't mean that you have to reconcile with the person if you choose not to. Forgiveness is about freeing yourself from the emotional burden of anger and bitterness.
- **Rebuilding Trust with Forgiveness**: Trust can be rebuilt, but it requires time, patience, and consistent effort. The person who betrayed you must demonstrate through their actions that they are trustworthy and committed to making amends. Small, consistent actions over time can help rebuild trust, but only if both parties are fully engaged in the process.

5. Rebuild Trust Gradually

Rebuilding trust after betrayal is a slow and deliberate process. Trust cannot be restored overnight, and it requires both parties to be patient and committed to the healing process.

- **Set Clear Boundaries**: In the aftermath of betrayal, setting boundaries is essential to rebuilding trust. Boundaries help protect your emotional well-being and create a framework for how the relationship will move forward. For example, you may set boundaries around communication, time spent together, or specific behaviors that need to change.
- **Be Transparent**: Rebuilding trust requires complete transparency from the person who betrayed you. This may involve being open about their actions, intentions, and emotions moving forward. Trust cannot be rebuilt if secrecy or dishonesty continues to be part of the relationship.
- **Acknowledge Progress**: As trust is gradually rebuilt, it's important to acknowledge the progress that has been made. Celebrating small victories—such as improved communication or consistent behavior—can reinforce the positive changes that are happening and provide encouragement to continue the process.

The Role of Apologies in Healing

A sincere apology is a crucial part of healing after betrayal. Apologies must go beyond just saying "I'm sorry"—they must demonstrate genuine remorse, accountability, and a commitment to change.

What Makes an Apology Effective?

1. **Take Full Responsibility**: The person who betrayed the trust must take full responsibility for their actions. This means acknowledging the hurt they caused without making excuses or blaming external factors.
2. **Express Genuine Remorse**: A heartfelt apology requires genuine remorse for the pain caused. The apology should not focus on defending or justifying the betrayal but on acknowledging the emotional impact it had on the other person.
3. **Offer a Plan for Change**: A meaningful apology also includes a commitment to change. This could involve specific actions to prevent the betrayal from happening again or a willingness to engage in open and honest communication moving forward.
4. **Be Patient with the Process**: An apology alone doesn't heal the wounds caused by betrayal. The person who betrayed the trust must be patient and understanding as the other person works through their feelings of hurt and betrayal.

Healing After Betrayal in Different Types of Relationships

While the steps to healing after betrayal are similar across different types of relationships, there are unique dynamics to consider in romantic, familial, friendship, and professional settings.

Healing Betrayal in Romantic Relationships

Betrayal in romantic relationships often involves infidelity, dishonesty, or emotional abandonment. Rebuilding trust in these relationships requires a renewed commitment to honesty, emotional intimacy, and transparency.

- **Infidelity**: Infidelity is one of the most common forms of betrayal in romantic relationships. Healing after infidelity requires both partners to address the underlying issues that led to the betrayal, as well as the emotional wounds caused by the affair. Open communication, counseling, and a renewed focus on building trust can help couples move forward, though it is not always possible to fully repair the relationship.

- **Emotional Betrayal**: Emotional betrayal, such as hiding feelings or forming emotional connections with others outside the relationship, can be just as damaging as physical betrayal. Rebuilding trust requires emotional openness and a commitment to rebuilding the emotional intimacy that was lost.

Healing Betrayal in Family Relationships

Betrayal in family relationships often involves broken promises, neglect, or unresolved conflicts that fester over time. Rebuilding trust in families requires patience, open dialogue, and a willingness to break generational cycles of mistrust.

- **Parent-Child Relationships**: Betrayal in parent-child relationships can leave deep emotional scars. Whether it's a broken promise, neglect, or a failure to provide support during difficult times, rebuilding trust between parents and children requires both parties to acknowledge the hurt and work toward healing through consistent support and open communication.
- **Sibling Relationships**: Sibling betrayal can take many forms, including rivalry, competition, or dishonesty. Healing after sibling betrayal requires a commitment to understanding each other's perspectives and rebuilding trust through shared accountability and mutual respect.

Healing Betrayal in Friendships

Friendships can be deeply affected by betrayal, especially if the betrayal involves dishonesty, gossip, or a breach of confidence. Rebuilding trust in friendships requires both parties to engage in honest communication and work toward rebuilding the emotional connection that was damaged.

· **Rebuilding After Dishonesty**: If a friend has been dishonest or has broken a confidence, trust can be rebuilt through open communication and a renewed commitment to transparency. It may also require setting new boundaries to prevent future betrayals.

Healing Betrayal in Professional Relationships

Betrayal in professional relationships can involve breaches of trust, such as taking credit for someone else's work, breaking confidentiality, or failing to follow through on commitments. Rebuilding trust in the workplace requires accountability, transparency, and a focus on restoring professional integrity.

· **Rebuilding Trust in Teams**: If a team member has betrayed the trust of their colleagues, rebuilding trust may involve group discussions, establishing clear expectations, and creating an environment where accountability and transparency are prioritized.

Conclusion: Moving Forward After Betrayal

Betrayal is one of the most painful experiences in any relationship, but it doesn't have to mark the end. With time, commitment, and a willingness to engage in honest communication, trust can be rebuilt. Whether the relationship is romantic, familial, friendly, or professional, healing after betrayal requires a shared effort from both parties to move forward with openness, accountability, and a commitment to change.

Rebuilding trust after betrayal is a slow process, but it is possible. And for some, it can lead to a stronger, more resilient relationship, where both parties are more aware of the importance of trust and are more committed to protecting it moving forward.

7

Chapter 7: Building Trust in Yourself

- *Why self-trust is the foundation of all other relationships*
- *Exercises to develop inner confidence and integrity*
- *How to align your actions with your values*

Trust in yourself is the foundation upon which all other forms of trust are built. Before you can fully trust others or rebuild trust after it's been broken, you must first learn to trust yourself. Self-trust is essential for personal growth, emotional resilience, and the ability to form healthy relationships. When you trust yourself, you are confident in your own judgment, decisions, and ability to handle challenges.

In this chapter, we will explore the importance of self-trust, the signs of a lack of self-trust, and practical strategies for building and maintaining self-trust. We will also discuss how self-trust affects your relationships with others and how to align your actions with your values.

Why Self-Trust is Crucial

Self-trust is the belief that you can rely on yourself to make sound decisions, navigate life's challenges, and honor your own needs and boundaries. It's about having confidence in your own judgment and abilities, as well as being kind and compassionate toward yourself when you make mistakes.

When you trust yourself, you are more resilient in the face of adversity because you know that, regardless of the outcome, you can rely on yourself to navigate difficult situations. This inner confidence also helps you maintain integrity and stay true to your values, even when external pressures or challenges arise.

The Role of Self-Trust in Relationships

Self-trust directly impacts your ability to build trust with others. If you don't trust yourself, it's difficult to trust others fully. You may constantly second-guess your decisions, doubt your ability to navigate conflicts, or fear that others will betray you because you lack confidence in your own judgment.

In contrast, when you trust yourself, you approach relationships with greater confidence and emotional security. You can set healthy boundaries, communicate openly, and make decisions that align with your values and needs. This self-assurance fosters deeper trust with others, as they sense that you are emotionally grounded and reliable.

Signs of a Lack of Self-Trust

Many people struggle with self-trust, often without realizing it. The following are common signs of a lack of self-trust:

1. Constant Self-Doubt

If you frequently second-guess your decisions or struggle to make choices, it may be a sign that you don't fully trust yourself. Self-doubt can cause you to rely heavily on others for validation or guidance, rather than trusting your own judgment.

2. Fear of Failure

A lack of self-trust often manifests as a fear of failure. You may avoid taking risks or trying new things because you don't believe in your ability to succeed or recover from setbacks. This fear can keep you stuck in your comfort zone, preventing personal growth and new experiences.

3. Difficulty Setting Boundaries

People who struggle with self-trust often find it difficult to set and enforce boundaries. They may prioritize others' needs over their own, fearing that asserting their boundaries will lead to conflict or rejection. This can result in feelings of resentment, burnout, and emotional exhaustion.

4. Seeking External Validation

If you rely heavily on others' approval or opinions to feel confident in your decisions, it may be a sign that you don't fully trust yourself. While it's normal to seek feedback from others, constantly needing external validation indicates a lack of confidence in your own judgment.

5. Overthinking and Indecisiveness

Overthinking every decision or being unable to make a choice without considering all possible outcomes can indicate a lack of self-trust. This can lead to paralysis by analysis, where you feel stuck and unable to move forward because you don't trust yourself to make the right choice.

How to Build Self-Trust

Building self-trust is a gradual process that involves strengthening your relationship with yourself, honoring your needs and boundaries, and developing confidence in your ability to navigate life's challenges. Here are practical strategies to help you build and maintain self-trust:

1. Keep Promises to Yourself

Just as trust is built with others by keeping promises and commitments, self-trust is built by following through on the promises you make to yourself. When you set a goal, no matter how small, make a commitment to achieving it. This could be as simple as sticking to a daily routine, completing a personal project, or taking time for self-care.

Every time you honor a commitment to yourself, you strengthen your self-trust. Conversely, when you frequently break promises to yourself—such as setting goals and not following through—you undermine your confidence in your own abilities.

2. Listen to Your Intuition

Your intuition is a powerful tool for decision-making, but many people ignore or dismiss it, particularly when it conflicts with external opinions. To build self-trust, practice listening to your inner voice and following your instincts, even when it feels uncomfortable.

Start by tuning in to your feelings and gut reactions when making decisions.

If something doesn't feel right, take time to reflect on why that might be. Trusting your intuition allows you to make decisions that align with your values and desires, rather than being swayed by external pressures.

3. Be Kind and Compassionate Toward Yourself

Self-compassion is an essential component of self-trust. When you make mistakes or experience setbacks, it's important to treat yourself with the same kindness and understanding that you would offer a friend. Rather than criticizing yourself for failures, acknowledge that mistakes are a natural part of life and an opportunity for growth.

By practicing self-compassion, you create a sense of emotional safety within yourself. This inner kindness allows you to take risks, pursue your goals, and trust that you can handle challenges without being overly harsh or self-critical.

4. Set and Enforce Boundaries

Setting boundaries is an important aspect of self-trust because it involves honoring your own needs and protecting your emotional well-being. To build self-trust, practice setting clear boundaries in your relationships, work, and personal life.

When you set a boundary, it's essential to enforce it consistently. This demonstrates to yourself that you are capable of standing up for your needs and protecting your mental and emotional health. Over time, this practice strengthens your self-confidence and reinforces your ability to trust your judgment.

5. Make Decisions with Confidence

One of the most powerful ways to build self-trust is to make decisions with confidence. While it's natural to experience doubt or uncertainty, trust yourself to make the best choice with the information available to you at the time.

If you struggle with decision-making, start with smaller, low-stakes decisions to build confidence. Over time, as you become more comfortable trusting your judgment, you'll find it easier to make larger decisions without overthinking or relying on others for validation.

Aligning Your Actions with Your Values

Self-trust is closely linked to living in alignment with your values. When your actions consistently reflect your core beliefs and principles, you build a sense of integrity and self-respect. This alignment strengthens self-trust because you know that, regardless of external circumstances, you are acting in accordance with what matters most to you.

Identifying Your Core Values

To build self-trust, it's important to clarify your core values—the beliefs and principles that guide your decisions and actions. These values might include honesty, compassion, integrity, or personal growth. Take time to reflect on what matters most to you and how these values influence your daily life.

Living in Alignment with Your Values

Once you've identified your core values, the next step is to ensure that your actions align with those values. This may involve making changes in your personal or professional life to better reflect your priorities. For example, if one of your core values is honesty, but you find yourself avoiding difficult conversations, it may be time to practice more open and direct communication.

By living in alignment with your values, you strengthen your sense of self-trust because you know that your actions are consistent with your beliefs. This integrity fosters confidence in your ability to navigate challenges and make decisions that honor your true self.

The Role of Self-Trust in Relationships

Self-trust not only benefits your personal growth but also enhances your relationships with others. When you trust yourself, you are more likely to set healthy boundaries, communicate openly, and build trust with others.

Setting Boundaries in Relationships

One of the most important ways that self-trust manifests in relationships is through boundary-setting. When you trust yourself, you feel confident in your ability to set and enforce boundaries that protect your emotional well-being. This may involve saying no to requests that don't align with your values, speaking up when you feel disrespected, or creating space for self-care.

Healthy boundaries not only protect your emotional health but also foster mutual respect in relationships. When others see that you value yourself and your needs, they are more likely to respect your boundaries and trust you in return.

Trusting Yourself to Navigate Conflict

Conflict is an inevitable part of any relationship, but trusting yourself to navigate conflict with honesty and integrity can strengthen your relationships. Self-trust allows you to approach conflict with confidence, knowing that you can express your needs and emotions without fear of rejection or abandonment.

When you trust yourself in conflict situations, you are more likely to communicate openly and assertively, rather than resorting to passive-aggressive behavior or avoiding the issue altogether. This openness fosters deeper trust with others, as they can rely on you to address issues directly and with respect.

Rebuilding Self-Trust After it's Broken

Just as trust with others can be broken, self-trust can also be damaged. This often happens when we make choices that go against our values, neglect our own needs, or break promises to ourselves. Fortunately, just like trust in relationships, self-trust can be rebuilt with time, effort, and intentional action.

Steps to Rebuild Self-Trust

1. **Acknowledge the Break**: The first step to rebuilding self-trust is to acknowledge where it has been broken. This might involve reflecting on moments when you ignored your intuition, failed to honor your boundaries, or neglected your own needs.

2. **Forgive Yourself**: Self-forgiveness is crucial for rebuilding trust. Just as you would forgive a friend who let you down, offer yourself the same grace and understanding. Acknowledge that mistakes are part of the learning process and that you are capable of growing and improving.

3. **Commit to Change**: Once you've acknowledged where your self-trust

has been broken, commit to making changes that align with your values and needs. This may involve setting new goals, creating healthier habits, or practicing better self-care.

4. **Follow Through on Promises**: Rebuilding self-trust requires consistent action. Start by setting small, achievable goals for yourself and following through on them. Each time you honor a commitment to yourself, you reinforce your ability to trust your own judgment and decisions.

5. **Celebrate Your Progress**: As you rebuild self-trust, take time to celebrate your progress. Recognize the small victories along the way, whether it's setting a boundary, following your intuition, or honoring a personal commitment.

Conclusion: The Power of Self-Trust

Self-trust is the foundation of personal growth, resilience, and strong relationships. When you trust yourself, you navigate life with greater confidence, integrity, and emotional security. Building self-trust is a lifelong process, but it is one that yields profound rewards—not only in your relationship with yourself but also in your connections with others.

By keeping promises to yourself, listening to your intuition, practicing self-compassion, and aligning your actions with your values, you can strengthen your self-trust and create a life that reflects your true self. With self-trust as your foundation, you are better equipped to build trust with others and create healthy, fulfilling relationships.

IV

Part 4: Sustaining Trust Over Time

In Part 4, we will explore how to sustain trust over time, particularly during difficult or uncertain times. We'll examine the role of daily practices in keeping trust alive, how personal growth affects trust, and how to navigate trust during life's most challenging moments.

8

Chapter 8: Trust as a Daily Practice

- ***How to maintain trust in long-term relationships***
- ***The importance of daily acts of trust***
- ***Recognizing the small moments that build trust***

Trust is not a one-time achievement; it is an ongoing process that requires consistent nurturing and care. Once trust has been built, the challenge becomes maintaining and sustaining it over the long term. Life is full of changes—whether it's personal growth, career shifts, family dynamics, or external challenges like financial stress or illness—and each of these can test the trust in a relationship. Understanding how to maintain trust during the normal ebbs and flows of life is crucial to ensuring that relationships remain strong and resilient.

Trust is built through small, consistent actions over time. While grand gestures and moments of reconciliation can be important, it's the day-to-day interactions that create the foundation of trust in any relationship. Trust, much like a garden, needs to be nurtured regularly to thrive. Neglecting trust in the everyday moments can lead to slow deterioration over time, eventually creating cracks in the relationship that are difficult to repair.

Let us now explore how trust is sustained through daily actions and how small gestures, consistency, and communication can reinforce trust every day. We will also look at how to recognize and celebrate the moments that strengthen trust, no matter how small they may seem.

The Importance of Daily Acts of Trust

Trust is often thought of as something that is built in dramatic moments—apologies after a fight, grand promises, or declarations of loyalty. While these moments do contribute to building trust, it's the smaller, everyday actions that create the steady foundation upon which trust is built. These daily acts of trust are often subtle and may even go unnoticed, but they play a critical role in sustaining trust over time.

Why Daily Trust Matters

1. **Consistency Reinforces Trust**: Every time you show up for your partner, friend, or family member in a predictable and reliable way, you reinforce the message that you are someone they can trust. These small moments add up, creating a sense of safety and reliability in the relationship.

2. **Small Acts Prevent Trust Erosion**: Trust isn't usually lost all at once. Instead, it erodes slowly when small acts of neglect, inconsistency, or dishonesty build up over time. By focusing on daily acts of trust, you prevent the slow erosion that can eventually lead to larger problems.

3. **Everyday Trust Builds Resilience**: When trust is built consistently over time, it creates a strong foundation that can help a relationship weather difficult moments. Relationships that have a strong foundation of everyday trust are more likely to survive challenges because both parties know they can rely on each other.

Practical Ways to Practice Trust Daily

Building trust in small, everyday moments doesn't require grand gestures or complex plans. It's about consistently showing up in ways that demonstrate reliability, honesty, and care. Here are practical ways to practice trust in your daily interactions:

1. Follow Through on Your Commitments

Whether it's something as simple as showing up on time for dinner or following through on a promise to take care of a task, keeping your word is one of the most fundamental ways to build trust. Each time you follow through on a commitment, no matter how small, you reinforce your reliability.

- **Examples**:
  - If you promise to pick up groceries on your way home, make sure you do it.
  - If you tell a friend you'll call them back later, make sure you make the call.

2. Be Present and Attentive

In today's fast-paced world, it's easy to be physically present but mentally distracted. Being fully present with your partner, friend, or family member— whether you're having a conversation, spending time together, or just sharing a quiet moment—signals that you value them and that they can trust you to be there for them.

- **Examples**:
  - Put your phone away during meals or conversations to give your full attention.
  - Actively listen when your partner is sharing something with you, without interrupting or multitasking.

3. Communicate Honestly and Openly

Honest communication is the backbone of trust. Being open about your thoughts, feelings, and intentions prevents misunderstandings and builds a strong sense of mutual trust. Even when the truth is uncomfortable, being honest fosters trust and prevents resentment from building up over time.

- **Examples**:
  - If you're feeling stressed or upset, communicate it to your partner rather than bottling it up.

- Share your thoughts and feelings regularly, so your partner knows what's going on in your life.

4. Show Appreciation and Gratitude

Expressing gratitude for the small things your partner, friend, or family member does strengthens trust by reinforcing the positive aspects of the relationship. When people feel appreciated, they are more likely to continue contributing to the relationship in meaningful ways.

- **Examples**:
- Thank your partner for cooking dinner, even if it's something they do every night.
- Acknowledge a friend's support during a tough time, no matter how small the gesture was.

5. Respect Boundaries

Honoring the boundaries of those you care about is a critical way to build trust. Whether it's respecting their need for space, their personal preferences, or their emotional limits, boundaries help to protect trust in a relationship.

- **Examples**:
- If your friend prefers not to discuss certain topics, respect that boundary without pushing them.
- If your partner needs alone time to recharge, give them the space they need without taking it personally.

6. Check In Regularly

Checking in with the people in your life shows that you care about their well-being and fosters a sense of connection. These small moments of connection help to sustain trust over time, especially during periods when life gets busy or stressful.

- **Examples**:
- Send a quick text to your partner during the day to see how they're doing.
- Make time for regular conversations with friends or family members, even if it's just a brief check-in.

Recognizing the Small Moments that Build Trust

In our relationships, we often focus on the big milestones—anniversaries, major decisions, or significant conflicts. However, it's important to recognize and celebrate the small, everyday moments that contribute to building trust. These moments are just as valuable and often more impactful in the long run.

Why Small Moments Matter

- **They Reinforce Reliability**: Each small act of trust—such as keeping a promise or being emotionally available—adds to the cumulative sense of reliability in the relationship.
- **They Create a Positive Feedback Loop**: When you recognize and appreciate the small ways that trust is built, you create a positive feedback loop that encourages more trust-building behaviors.
- **They Prevent Resentment**: Failing to recognize the small acts of trust can lead to feelings of being taken for granted, which can erode trust over time. Acknowledging these moments prevents resentment from building up.

How to Recognize and Celebrate Small Moments

1. **Express Appreciation for Small Acts**: Acknowledge the small things your partner or friend does, even if they seem routine. This could be thanking them for listening, appreciating their consistency, or recognizing their emotional support.
2. **Reflect on Daily Trust-Building Moments**: At the end of the day, take a moment to reflect on the small moments of trust that occurred throughout the day. This could be as simple as remembering a conversation

where both parties were honest and open.

3. **Celebrate Consistency**: If someone in your life consistently shows up for you, whether emotionally or physically, take time to celebrate that consistency. Trust isn't just about grand gestures; it's about showing up consistently over time.

Maintaining Trust in Long-Term Relationships

In long-term relationships, sustaining trust requires ongoing effort and attention. As time goes on, it can be easy to take trust for granted or to let small issues slide. However, maintaining trust in long-term relationships is essential for keeping the connection strong and preventing the buildup of unresolved issues.

Strategies for Maintaining Trust in Long-Term Relationships

1. **Continue to Prioritize Communication**: Even in long-term relationships, it's important to communicate openly and honestly. Don't assume that your partner knows what you're thinking or feeling—make a habit of sharing your thoughts and emotions regularly.

2. **Avoid Complacency**: Trust can erode over time if it's not actively nurtured. Avoid becoming complacent in your relationship by continuing to invest in the relationship through small acts of love, appreciation, and trust-building.

3. **Address Issues Promptly**: In long-term relationships, it's easy to let small issues slide, but over time, these small issues can build up and create larger problems. Make it a point to address issues as they arise, rather than letting them fester.

4. **Be Consistent Over Time**: Trust in long-term relationships is built through consistency. Continue to show up for your partner, keep your promises, and be emotionally available, even as life changes and evolves.

The Role of Rituals and Traditions in Sustaining Trust

Rituals and traditions—whether they are daily, weekly, or yearly—play an important role in sustaining trust over time. These rituals create a sense of stability and predictability in the relationship, which reinforces trust.

Examples of Trust-Building Rituals

1. **Daily Check-Ins**: Set aside time each day to check in with your partner or family members, even if it's just for a few minutes. This consistent connection helps to build and maintain trust.

2. **Weekly Rituals**: Create a weekly ritual, such as a date night or family dinner, where you can reconnect and spend quality time together. These rituals help to maintain the bond and reinforce trust over time.

3. **Yearly Traditions**: Whether it's celebrating anniversaries, birthdays, or holidays, yearly traditions create opportunities to reflect on the relationship and strengthen trust through shared experiences.

Conclusion: Trust is a Lifelong Practice

Trust is not something that is built once and then left alone. It is a lifelong practice that requires ongoing effort, attention, and care. By focusing on daily acts of trust, communicating openly, and recognizing the small moments that build trust, you can sustain trust in your relationships over time.

In the next chapter, we will explore how trust evolves alongside personal growth and life changes, and how to maintain trust when both individuals in a relationship are growing and changing.

9

Chapter 9: Trust and Personal Growth

- *How trust evolves as individuals grow and change*
- *Navigating personal growth within relationships*
- *How to foster trust during life transitions*

Personal growth is a natural and essential part of life. As individuals, we are constantly evolving—whether through career changes, new experiences, shifts in values, or emotional and psychological development. While growth is a positive and necessary part of being human, it can also create challenges in relationships. As people grow, their priorities, desires, and outlook on life may change, which can sometimes put strain on the trust that exists between them and others.

In this chapter, we'll explore how trust and personal growth intersect in relationships. We'll examine how to maintain trust when both individuals are growing and changing, how to navigate the challenges that personal growth can create, and how to foster trust while allowing for mutual development within a relationship.

The Dynamic Nature of Trust and Growth

Trust, like relationships, is not static. It evolves and adapts as people grow. When individuals in a relationship are growing—whether emotionally, intellectually, or professionally—their needs, expectations, and priorities may shift. These changes can test the trust within the relationship, especially if the growth is uneven or if one partner feels left behind.

However, trust can also be strengthened by personal growth. As individuals develop a deeper understanding of themselves, they often become more emotionally mature, better communicators, and more empathetic. This growth can lead to greater trust if both parties are committed to supporting each other's development and navigating changes together.

Why Growth Can Challenge Trust

1. **Shifting Priorities**: As people grow, their priorities may change. What was once important in the relationship—such as shared hobbies, routines, or life goals—may no longer hold the same value. These shifts can create feelings of distance or misalignment between partners.

2. **Fear of Growing Apart**: One of the most common fears in relationships is the idea that personal growth will lead to growing apart. When one person embarks on a journey of self-improvement or personal development, the other may fear that they will be left behind or that the relationship will no longer be compatible.

3. **Insecurity and Jealousy**: Personal growth can sometimes trigger feelings of insecurity or jealousy in a partner, especially if they feel that their own growth is stagnating. This insecurity can erode trust if it leads to feelings of inadequacy or fear of being replaced.

4. **Communication Breakdown**: As individuals grow, they may develop new interests, perspectives, or values. If these changes are not communicated effectively, it can create misunderstandings or a sense of emotional distance, which can weaken trust.

Navigating Personal Growth Together

While personal growth can present challenges, it is also an opportunity for individuals to deepen their connection and strengthen trust. The key is to navigate growth together, supporting each other's development while maintaining open communication and mutual respect.

1. Communicate Your Growth and Changes

One of the most important aspects of navigating personal growth in a relationship is communication. As you grow and evolve, it's essential to share your journey with your partner, friend, or family member. This doesn't mean that you have to agree on every new perspective or interest, but it does mean that you should be open about the changes you're experiencing.

- **Examples**:
  - If you've recently developed a new passion for a hobby, share your excitement with your partner and invite them to explore it with you, even if it's something they're not initially interested in.
  - If your values or goals are shifting, have a conversation about how those changes might impact your relationship and how you can adapt together.

2. Support Each Other's Growth

One of the most important ways to maintain trust during personal growth is to actively support each other's development. This support can take many forms—emotional encouragement, practical assistance, or simply being a sounding board as the other person navigates new challenges.

Supporting your partner or friend through their growth fosters trust because it shows that you are invested in their well-being and success. It also reassures them that you are not threatened by their growth but are instead excited to see them flourish.

- **Examples**:
  - Encourage your partner to pursue new opportunities, such as going back to school, starting a business, or taking on a new hobby, even if it means temporary changes in your routine.
  - Offer emotional support during periods of personal growth, such as career transitions or personal challenges, by being patient and understanding as they navigate the changes.

3. Embrace Change as Part of the Relationship

Change is inevitable in any relationship, but how you respond to that change is what determines whether trust will be strengthened or weakened. Rather than fearing change, embrace it as a natural part of the relationship. Understand that growth, both individually and as a couple, is essential for the long-term health of any partnership.

- **Examples**:
- Recognize that as you grow, your relationship may need to adapt. This could mean renegotiating roles, expectations, or routines to accommodate the new dynamics.
- Be open to evolving together, rather than holding on to past versions of yourself or your partner. Allow the relationship to grow with you.

4. Cultivate Mutual Respect for Individual Journeys

One of the most important aspects of navigating personal growth in a relationship is cultivating mutual respect for each person's individual journey. You may not always be on the same path at the same time, and that's okay. The key is to respect and support each other's growth, even when it takes different forms.

Mutual respect fosters trust because it creates an environment where both individuals feel valued for who they are and where they are in their journey. It also prevents feelings of resentment or competition, which can arise when one person's growth is seen as threatening to the relationship.

- **Examples**:
- If your partner or friend is pursuing a new passion that doesn't interest you, respect their enthusiasm and support their efforts, even if it's not something you personally connect with.
- Avoid comparing your growth to that of your partner or friend. Everyone's journey is different, and growth happens at different paces for different people.

Trust During Life Transitions

Major life transitions—such as moving to a new city, changing careers, becoming parents, or experiencing loss—can be particularly challenging for trust in relationships. These transitions often bring about significant changes in routines, priorities, and emotional needs, all of which can test the trust that has been built over time.

How Transitions Can Challenge Trust

1. **Increased Stress**: Life transitions often come with increased stress, which can strain relationships and test trust. For example, moving to a new city or starting a new job can create feelings of uncertainty or overwhelm, making it difficult to maintain the same level of emotional connection.
2. **Changing Roles**: Transitions such as becoming parents or taking on a new leadership role at work can change the dynamics of a relationship, shifting roles and responsibilities. These changes can create tension if they are not communicated and navigated thoughtfully.
3. **Time and Attention**: During life transitions, the demands on your time and attention may shift, leaving less time for nurturing the relationship. This can create feelings of neglect or distance if not addressed openly.

Maintaining Trust During Life Transitions

Navigating life transitions requires flexibility, patience, and a commitment to maintaining trust, even when things feel uncertain. Here are some strategies for maintaining trust during times of transition:

1. Communicate Early and Often

During times of change, communication is more important than ever. Make a conscious effort to check in with each other regularly, discussing how the transition is affecting both individuals and the relationship.

- **Examples**:
- If you're moving to a new city, have open conversations about how the move will impact your routines, your relationship, and your emotional well-being. Discuss any fears or concerns early on, rather than waiting until stress builds up.
- If you're starting a new job, make time to talk about how the new schedule or responsibilities will affect your time together, and set expectations for how to stay connected.

2. Be Patient with Each Other's Adjustments

Life transitions often require both individuals to make adjustments, whether it's adapting to a new routine, learning new roles, or handling increased stress. Patience is key to maintaining trust during these times. Recognize that both people may be feeling the strain of the transition, and give each other the space and time to adjust.

- **Examples**:
- If your partner is struggling with a career transition, be patient and offer support without pressure. Understand that it may take time for them to find their footing in the new role.
- If you're both adjusting to a new life stage, such as becoming parents, be patient with each other as you navigate the learning curve together.

3. Stay Emotionally Available

One of the biggest challenges during life transitions is staying emotionally available to each other. Even when time is limited or stress is high, it's important to prioritize emotional connection and support.

- **Examples**:
- Make time for emotional check-ins, even if it's just a few minutes each day, to discuss how you're feeling and how the transition is affecting you.
- Offer emotional support by listening without judgment, being empathetic, and validating each other's experiences during the transition.

Personal Growth Within Long-Term Relationships

In long-term relationships, personal growth can sometimes create a sense of imbalance, particularly if one partner is growing in a way that the other isn't. However, with open communication, mutual support, and a commitment to growing together, personal development can actually enhance long-term relationships by fostering deeper understanding and emotional intimacy.

Supporting Growth in Long-Term Relationships

1. **Celebrate Each Other's Growth**: When your partner or friend experiences personal growth, celebrate their achievements and support their development. This reinforces trust by showing that you are invested in their success and happiness.

2. **Grow Together, Not Apart**: While personal growth is an individual journey, it's important to find ways to grow together in a long-term relationship. This could mean setting shared goals, exploring new experiences together, or finding ways to integrate each person's growth into the relationship.

3. **Adapt to New Dynamics**: As both individuals grow, the dynamics of the relationship may shift. Be open to adapting the relationship to accommodate these changes, whether that means renegotiating roles, finding new ways to connect, or creating space for individual pursuits.

Conclusion: Embracing Growth and Trust Together

Personal growth is an inevitable part of life, and when approached with openness and mutual respect, it can strengthen trust in relationships. By communicating openly, supporting each other's development, and navigating life transitions together, trust can evolve and deepen alongside individual growth.

In the next chapter, we will explore how to maintain trust during times of uncertainty, such as illness, financial struggles, or other external challenges. These periods can test the strength of trust in relationships, but with the right approach, they can also bring people closer together.

10

Chapter 10: Trust in Times of Uncertainty

- *How to maintain trust during difficult or uncertain times (illness, financial struggles, etc.)*
- *Strategies for building trust when external factors are out of your control*

Life is full of unexpected events and challenges—illness, financial struggles, job loss, natural disasters, and global crises. These moments of uncertainty can test the trust in any relationship, often pushing it to its limits. Uncertainty breeds fear, anxiety, and stress, all of which can erode trust if not managed properly. However, with the right strategies, trust can not only survive but also thrive during times of uncertainty.

In this chapter, we'll explore how trust is maintained and strengthened during periods of uncertainty, crisis, and upheaval. We'll look at how to navigate these difficult moments together, how to communicate effectively when emotions run high, and how to foster resilience in relationships during trying times.

The Impact of Uncertainty on Trust

Uncertainty has a unique ability to bring underlying issues in relationships to the surface. When life feels unpredictable, and the future is unclear, the stability of relationships can be called into question. During these times, trust is often tested in the following ways:

1. Increased Stress and Anxiety

Times of uncertainty are often accompanied by heightened stress and anxiety, which can make it difficult for individuals to remain calm, patient, and emotionally available. This heightened emotional state can lead to misunderstandings, miscommunications, and overreactions, all of which can weaken trust in a relationship.

- **Example**: During a financial crisis, one partner may feel anxious about money, leading to arguments or tension over spending habits. This stress can cause a breakdown in communication, eroding trust between the partners.

2. Shifts in Roles and Responsibilities

In times of crisis, the roles and responsibilities within a relationship may shift dramatically. For example, if one partner becomes ill or loses their job, the other may need to take on more responsibilities, both financially and emotionally. These shifts can create imbalances that strain the relationship and lead to resentment if not managed properly.

- **Example**: If one partner is unable to contribute financially due to job loss, they may feel insecure or guilty, while the other partner may feel burdened by the increased responsibilities. If these feelings aren't communicated openly, they can lead to distrust and emotional distance.

3. Fear of the Unknown

Uncertainty naturally triggers fear—fear of the future, fear of loss, fear of failure. This fear can cause individuals to act defensively, withdraw emotionally, or project their anxieties onto their partner, leading to a breakdown in trust.

- **Example**: During a health crisis, one partner may become withdrawn and emotionally distant, not wanting to burden the other with their fears. This emotional withdrawal can create feelings of isolation and distrust in the relationship.

Maintaining Trust During Uncertainty

While uncertainty can strain relationships, it can also provide an opportunity to strengthen trust. Navigating difficult times together can bring partners, friends, and family members closer, as they learn to rely on each other for support and comfort. Here are some key strategies for maintaining trust during times of uncertainty:

1. Communicate Openly and Honestly

In moments of uncertainty, open and honest communication is more important than ever. When life feels unpredictable, it's essential to create a space where both individuals feel comfortable expressing their fears, anxieties, and concerns without judgment.

- **How to Practice Open Communication**:
- **Share Your Fears**: Don't be afraid to admit when you're feeling scared or uncertain. Sharing your fears can help your partner understand what you're going through and provide emotional support.
- **Be Honest About Your Needs**: During times of uncertainty, your needs may change. Whether it's emotional support, financial assistance, or simply space to process your emotions, be clear about what you need from your partner or loved one.
- **Avoid Bottling Up Emotions**: Bottling up emotions during a crisis can lead to emotional distance and resentment. Make it a priority to talk about your feelings regularly, even if the conversations are difficult.

2. Be Empathetic and Patient

Uncertainty affects everyone differently. Some people may become more anxious or withdrawn, while others may cope by becoming more controlling or irritable. It's important to practice empathy and patience with your partner or loved one during these times, recognizing that they may be processing the situation in their own way.

- **How to Show Empathy and Patience**:
- **Validate Their Feelings**: Let your partner know that their feelings are valid, even if they react to the situation differently than you do. For example, if your partner is more anxious than you, acknowledge their fears rather than dismissing them.
- **Give Them Space if Needed**: Some people need time alone to process their emotions during uncertain times. If your partner or loved one needs space, respect their boundaries while reassuring them that you're available when they're ready to talk.
- **Be Patient with Emotional Reactions**: Stress and anxiety can cause people to act out of character. Be patient with any emotional outbursts or irritability, and try to understand where those emotions are coming from rather than taking them personally.

3. Stay United as a Team

One of the most important aspects of maintaining trust during uncertainty is reinforcing the idea that you are a team. No matter what challenges arise, remind each other that you are in this together and that you will face the uncertainty as a united front.

- **How to Stay United**:
- **Make Joint Decisions**: Whether it's financial decisions, medical choices, or major life changes, involve each other in the decision-making process. This reinforces the idea that you're working together and that both voices matter.
- **Create a Plan Together**: During uncertain times, having a plan—no matter how simple—can provide a sense of stability. Sit down together and create a plan for how you will manage the situation, whether it's a financial crisis or a health issue. This helps both parties feel empowered and involved.
- **Use "We" Language**: Frame conversations around how "we" will handle

the situation, rather than focusing on individual worries or responsibilities. This reinforces the idea that you are facing the challenges as a team.

4. Be Transparent and Honest About the Situation

Transparency is critical during times of uncertainty. Whether it's financial difficulties, a health issue, or any other crisis, being upfront about the reality of the situation prevents misunderstandings and builds trust.

How to Practice Transparency:

- **Be Open About the Facts**: If you're facing a financial crisis, for example, be honest about the numbers and the impact it will have. Hiding information to protect the other person can backfire if they later discover the full extent of the situation.
- **Discuss Worst-Case Scenarios**: While it's important to remain hopeful, discussing worst-case scenarios can help both parties feel prepared. This transparency builds trust by showing that you are willing to face even the most difficult truths together.
- **Avoid Keeping Secrets**: In times of uncertainty, it can be tempting to hide information or downplay the severity of a situation to avoid worrying the other person. However, this can lead to a breakdown in trust if the truth eventually comes out.

5. Show Emotional Availability

During times of uncertainty, emotional availability is essential. Even if you're both feeling stressed or anxious, making an effort to be emotionally present for each other strengthens trust and provides comfort.

- **How to Be Emotionally Available**:
- **Offer Comfort**: Sometimes, the best way to support someone during uncertainty is simply by being there. Offer physical comfort, such as a hug or a reassuring touch, and emotional support by listening without judgment.
- **Make Time for Connection**: Set aside time each day to check in with

each other emotionally. This could be as simple as sitting down for a few minutes to talk about how you're feeling or sharing a quiet moment together.

- **Validate Their Emotions**: If your partner is feeling overwhelmed, validate their emotions rather than trying to fix the situation. Let them know that it's okay to feel anxious or uncertain, and offer your support in any way you can.

Trust and Resilience in Relationships

Resilience is the ability to bounce back from adversity, and in relationships, it's an essential quality for maintaining trust during difficult times. Building resilience in your relationship helps you navigate uncertainty with greater confidence and trust in each other.

1. Strengthen Emotional Resilience

Emotional resilience involves managing stress, adapting to change, and maintaining emotional balance during difficult times. In relationships, emotional resilience allows both partners to cope with uncertainty without losing trust in each other.

- **How to Strengthen Emotional Resilience**:
- **Practice Stress-Management Techniques**: Develop healthy ways to manage stress, such as mindfulness, meditation, exercise, or talking to a trusted friend. When both individuals are emotionally balanced, it's easier to maintain trust.
- **Focus on the Present**: Uncertainty often involves worrying about the future, which can create unnecessary stress. Practice focusing on the present moment and what you can control right now, rather than worrying about what might happen in the future.
- **Cultivate Optimism**: While it's important to acknowledge the challenges of uncertainty, maintaining a hopeful outlook helps both individuals stay emotionally resilient. Cultivate optimism by focusing on the positives in the relationship and the strengths you both bring to the table.

2. Build Problem-Solving Skills Together

During times of uncertainty, strong problem-solving skills are essential. When both individuals can work together to solve problems, it strengthens trust and helps the relationship navigate challenges more effectively.

- **How to Build Problem-Solving Skills**:
- **Collaborate on Solutions**: When faced with a challenge, work together to brainstorm solutions. Even if you don't immediately find the perfect answer, the act of collaborating reinforces trust and teamwork.
- **Stay Calm Under Pressure**: Problem-solving requires a clear head. When stress runs high, take a moment to breathe and regroup before tackling the issue. Staying calm under pressure helps maintain trust and prevents rash decisions.
- **Be Flexible**: Uncertainty often requires adapting and changing plans as new information arises. Stay flexible in your problem-solving approach, and be willing to adjust your strategies as needed.

The Role of Trust in Recovering from Crisis

While uncertainty can strain relationships, it can also provide an opportunity for growth and healing. When trust is maintained during difficult times, it strengthens the relationship's ability to recover and thrive once the crisis has passed.

1. Reflect on the Experience

After navigating a period of uncertainty, take time to reflect on the experience together. Discuss what you learned, how you grew as a couple or family, and how the crisis brought you closer.

- **How to Reflect Together**:
- **Acknowledge the Challenges**: Be honest about the difficulties you faced and how they impacted the relationship. This reflection helps you both understand what worked and what could be improved for future challenges.

- **Celebrate Your Resilience**: Reflect on the ways you both showed resilience and supported each other during the crisis. Celebrating your strengths reinforces trust and helps you feel more confident in your ability to handle future challenges.

2. Reaffirm Your Commitment

After weathering a period of uncertainty together, reaffirm your commitment to each other and to the relationship. This reaffirmation reinforces the trust that was built during the crisis and provides a sense of stability moving forward.

- **How to Reaffirm Commitment**:
- **Express Gratitude**: Thank each other for the support, patience, and understanding shown during the difficult time. Expressing gratitude reinforces the bond between you and deepens trust.
- **Set New Goals**: After navigating a crisis, setting new goals together can provide a sense of hope and direction for the future. These goals may be related to the relationship itself or to personal or professional growth.

Conclusion: Trust as the Anchor in Uncertainty

Trust is the anchor that keeps relationships grounded during times of uncertainty. By communicating openly, supporting each other emotionally, and working together as a team, trust can not only survive but thrive during difficult moments. These periods of uncertainty, while challenging, provide an opportunity for growth, resilience, and deeper connection.

In the next chapter, we'll explore how to rebuild trust in a world where trust in institutions and societal structures is often shaken. We'll look at how personal trust and community trust intersect, and how to navigate a world where trust seems increasingly fragile.

11

Chapter 11: Rebuilding Trust in a Broken World

- *How to maintain personal trust when societal or institutional trust is shaken?*
- *The importance of trust in community and society*
- *Strategies for rebuilding trust in larger systems*

In today's world, trust in many institutions—governments, media, corporations, even social systems—has been eroded by scandals, misinformation, and widespread disillusionment. As trust in larger societal structures weakens, individuals often struggle to navigate personal relationships, workplaces, and communities where trust feels fragile or broken. Rebuilding trust in a world that seems increasingly divided and uncertain requires both a personal and collective effort.

In this chapter, we'll explore how to rebuild trust in a world where mistrust is prevalent. We will look at how personal trust and societal trust intersect, the impact of broken trust on communities and relationships, and practical strategies for fostering trust in an increasingly complex and often fractured world.

The Crisis of Trust in the Modern World

Trust in institutions has been steadily declining for decades. A range of factors—political polarization, economic inequality, social media misinformation, corporate scandals, and public health crises—has contributed to an atmosphere of skepticism and distrust. People are questioning the credibility of leaders, organizations, and even their communities at a deeper level than ever before.

This widespread loss of trust has personal consequences. When trust in societal systems is broken, it can lead to feelings of insecurity, fear, and isolation. People may become more guarded in their personal relationships, more cynical about the world around them, and less willing to engage in community-building efforts.

How Broken Trust in Society Affects Individuals

1. **Erosion of Social Cohesion**: When trust in societal institutions is broken, it can lead to a breakdown in social cohesion. Communities may become more fragmented, with individuals retreating into smaller, more insular groups. This makes it harder for people to connect with others and fosters a sense of isolation.

2. **Increased Fear and Cynicism**: Widespread mistrust often leads to fear and cynicism. People may begin to see the world as a hostile place where they cannot rely on others, which in turn can make it harder to build trust in personal relationships.

3. **Impact on Personal Relationships**: When people feel betrayed by the systems they once trusted, it can spill over into their personal relationships. They may become more guarded, less open to vulnerability, and less willing to trust others, even in close relationships.

4. **Loss of Hope in Change**: When institutional trust is lost, it's common for people to feel powerless to enact change. This sense of helplessness can lead to disengagement from political or community activities, further eroding collective trust and making it harder to rebuild.

The Intersection of Personal and Societal Trust

Personal trust and societal trust are deeply interconnected. When people feel betrayed by the larger structures they once relied on, such as governments, corporations, or social systems, it can affect how they view trust at a more personal level. Conversely, when individuals practice trust-building behaviors in their personal lives and communities, they can contribute to restoring trust on a broader scale.

How Personal Trust Strengthens Societal Trust

1. **Trust Begins at the Individual Level**: Trust in larger systems starts with trust between individuals. When people feel that they can rely on those closest to them—family, friends, and colleagues—they are more likely to feel confident in their ability to navigate the broader societal challenges.

2. **Community Trust is Built Through Relationships**: Local communities thrive when people trust one another. Neighbors helping neighbors, local businesses supporting their customers, and community groups advocating for common causes all contribute to a sense of shared trust that strengthens the social fabric.

3. **Trustworthy Leadership**: Trustworthy leaders—whether in personal, local, or professional spheres—can inspire others to trust in the systems they represent. When individuals practice integrity, transparency, and empathy in their roles, they help to rebuild trust not only in themselves but in the larger systems they are part of.

Rebuilding Trust in Communities and Society

While rebuilding societal trust may seem like an overwhelming task, it often begins with small, intentional efforts within local communities and personal relationships. By focusing on rebuilding trust in our immediate environments, we can create a ripple effect that influences larger societal structures over time.

1. Practice Transparency and Accountability

One of the primary reasons trust in institutions has been eroded is the lack of transparency and accountability. When individuals and organizations hide information, fail to admit mistakes, or refuse to take responsibility for their actions, trust is quickly lost. Rebuilding trust requires a commitment to transparency and accountability at every level—whether in personal relationships, workplaces, or community organizations.

- **How to Practice Transparency**:
- **Be Open About Mistakes**: Whether in a personal or professional setting, openly acknowledge when mistakes are made. Admitting errors and taking responsibility builds trust by showing that you value honesty and accountability.
- **Share Information Freely**: In workplaces, community groups, and relationships, share information openly and avoid withholding important details. When people feel they are being kept in the dark, trust quickly erodes.
- **Follow Through on Promises**: Accountability means keeping your word. If you make a commitment, whether to a friend, family member, or colleague, ensure that you follow through. This reliability reinforces trust.

2. Foster Empathy and Understanding Across Differences

A major challenge in rebuilding trust in today's world is the deep polarization that exists across political, social, and cultural lines. Bridging these divides requires empathy and a willingness to understand perspectives that differ from your own. By fostering empathy and encouraging open dialogue, trust can be rebuilt across communities, even when opinions and values differ.

- **How to Foster Empathy**:
- **Listen Without Judgment**: When engaging with someone whose views differ from your own, listen with an open mind. Avoid jumping to conclusions or dismissing their perspective without fully hearing them

out.

- **Seek Common Ground**: Focus on shared values and goals, even when differences exist. Finding common ground helps to build trust by emphasizing what unites rather than what divides.
- **Encourage Civil Discourse**: In both personal and public settings, promote respectful conversations, especially when discussing controversial topics. Civil discourse fosters understanding and trust by creating a safe space for diverse opinions.

3. Build Trust Through Collective Action

One of the most effective ways to rebuild trust in communities is through collective action. When people come together to work toward a common goal— whether it's addressing local issues, supporting vulnerable populations, or advocating for systemic change—they strengthen the bonds of trust between individuals and groups.

- **Examples of Collective Action**:
- **Community Projects**: Volunteer for or organize community projects that bring people together to improve the local environment or support those in need. Whether it's a community clean-up, a food drive, or a local advocacy group, collective action fosters trust by showing that people can rely on each other.
- **Grassroots Movements**: Support or participate in grassroots movements that aim to address social injustices or advocate for political change. These movements often build trust by empowering individuals to take action and contribute to meaningful change.
- **Corporate Social Responsibility**: In workplaces, advocate for corporate social responsibility initiatives that give back to the community. When businesses engage in ethical practices and support local causes, they help rebuild trust in the corporate sector.

4. Lead with Integrity and Authenticity

Whether you're in a leadership position or simply leading by example in your personal relationships, acting with integrity is key to rebuilding trust. People are more likely to trust those who are authentic, transparent, and consistent in their words and actions.

- **How to Lead with Integrity**:
- **Be Authentic**: Authenticity builds trust by showing that you are genuine in your intentions. Avoid trying to be something you're not or pretending to have all the answers. Authenticity creates an environment where others feel safe to trust you.
- **Maintain Consistency**: Trust is built through consistency over time. Ensure that your actions align with your words and that you consistently uphold your values, both in personal relationships and professional settings.
- **Admit When You Don't Know**: People trust leaders who are honest about their limitations. If you don't have an answer, admit it and commit to finding one. This humility fosters trust by showing that you value truth over ego.

The Role of Trust in Healing a Divided Society

Rebuilding trust in a divided society requires more than just individual actions—it requires a collective commitment to healing the wounds caused by polarization, inequality, and injustice. Trust can only be rebuilt when people feel that they are being treated fairly, that their voices are being heard, and that those in power are acting with integrity and empathy.

1. Address Inequality and Injustice

One of the major reasons trust has eroded in many societies is the persistent inequality and injustice experienced by marginalized groups. Trust cannot be rebuilt without addressing these systemic issues head-on. This requires both acknowledging the harm that has been done and taking meaningful steps to create a more equitable society.

- **How to Address Inequality**:
- **Support Policies that Promote Equity**: Advocate for policies and practices that address racial, economic, and social inequality. This could include supporting affordable housing initiatives, criminal justice reform, or educational equity programs.
- **Listen to Marginalized Voices**: Rebuilding trust requires amplifying the voices of those who have been historically marginalized. Listen to their experiences, support their leadership, and prioritize their needs in collective decision-making.
- **Take Personal Responsibility**: Even if you are not in a position of power, you can contribute to rebuilding trust by taking personal responsibility for your actions. Educate yourself on issues of inequality and work to address any biases or behaviors that contribute to injustice.

2. Build Bridges Across Divides

In a world that often feels divided, it's important to actively seek out opportunities to build bridges across those divides. Whether through personal relationships, community work, or professional collaborations, creating opportunities for dialogue and collaboration can help rebuild trust and foster unity.

- **How to Build Bridges**:
- **Engage in Cross-Community Dialogue**: Participate in or organize events that bring together people from different backgrounds, cultures, or political affiliations. These dialogues create opportunities for understanding and trust-building.
- **Collaborate Across Differences**: In your workplace, community, or social groups, look for opportunities to collaborate with individuals or organizations that represent different perspectives. Working together on shared goals fosters trust by emphasizing commonalities.
- **Challenge Polarization**: Actively work to challenge the polarization that divides communities. This could involve speaking out against divisive rhetoric, promoting inclusive practices, or supporting initiatives that

bring people together.

Conclusion: Rebuilding Trust, One Step at a Time

Rebuilding trust in a broken world is not an easy task, but it is possible. It requires a commitment to transparency, empathy, collective action, and leadership with integrity. By focusing on rebuilding trust in our personal relationships, communities, and institutions, we can create a ripple effect that strengthens trust at a broader societal level.

Each step we take—whether through fostering empathy, promoting accountability, or addressing inequality—contributes to the slow but steady rebuilding of trust. While the challenges are significant, the rewards are profound: a more connected, compassionate, and resilient society where people feel safe to trust one another again.

12

Chapter 12: The Future of Trust

- *The evolving nature of trust in a digital age*
- *How technology impacts trust in relationships*
- *Future trends: What will trust look like in the years to come?*

As we move deeper into the 21st century, the concept of trust is evolving rapidly. In a world increasingly driven by technology, globalization, and constant connectivity, trust is being redefined in ways that are both exciting and challenging. The rise of artificial intelligence, social media, virtual interactions, and shifting cultural norms have brought new opportunities for connection and collaboration but have also raised significant questions about privacy, security, and the role of trust in a digital world.

In this final chapter, we'll explore how trust is changing in the digital age, the impact of technology on trust in relationships, and what the future of trust may look like in an increasingly interconnected world. We'll also examine the challenges and opportunities that come with building trust in a world where human interactions are increasingly mediated by technology.

The Role of Technology in Shaping Trust

Technology has fundamentally transformed how we interact with one another. From social media platforms that allow us to connect with people across the globe to online marketplaces that enable us to conduct business without ever meeting face-to-face, technology has created new spaces for building trust—and for eroding it.

1. Trust in Digital Relationships

Digital relationships, whether personal or professional, are becoming increasingly common. We form friendships, business partnerships, and even romantic relationships online. In these digital spaces, trust is often built through words and actions without the benefit of physical presence or face-to-face interaction.

- **Opportunities for Trust**: Technology allows people to connect in ways that were previously impossible, creating opportunities for new kinds of relationships. Online communities, social media groups, and professional networks offer spaces where trust can be built across geographic and cultural boundaries.
- **Challenges to Trust**: However, the anonymity of the internet can also make it easier for trust to be broken. The rise of online scams, catfishing, and misinformation has made it harder to trust digital interactions, as it can be difficult to verify a person's identity or intentions.

2. Trust in Virtual Workplaces

The COVID-19 pandemic accelerated the shift toward remote and virtual work, fundamentally changing how trust is built and maintained in professional settings. In virtual workplaces, trust is built not through casual office conversations or face-to-face meetings but through virtual communication, collaboration tools, and digital accountability.

- **Building Trust in Remote Teams**: In virtual work environments, trust is built through consistent communication, transparency, and accountability. Video calls, instant messaging, and project management tools have become essential for maintaining trust in remote teams. Leaders must foster a culture of trust by being accessible, transparent, and supportive of their remote employees.

- **Challenges in Virtual Trust**: One of the biggest challenges in building trust in virtual workplaces is the lack of physical presence. Without in-person interactions, it can be harder to establish rapport, read body language, or address misunderstandings quickly. Remote teams must work harder to maintain trust through clear communication and consistent follow-through.

The Impact of Social Media on Trust

Social media has revolutionized how people communicate and build relationships, but it has also introduced new complexities when it comes to trust. Platforms like Facebook, Twitter, Instagram, and TikTok have made it easier than ever to connect with others, share experiences, and form online communities. However, the very nature of social media can also create environments where trust is easily manipulated or broken.

1. The Double-Edged Sword of Social Media

- **Building Connection and Trust**: Social media allows people to connect with others who share their interests, values, and experiences, creating opportunities to build trust across geographic and cultural boundaries. Many friendships, professional relationships, and even romantic partnerships begin online, with social media serving as the initial point of connection.
- **Misinformation and Distrust**: However, social media is also a breeding ground for misinformation, fake news, and deceptive practices. The ability to curate a carefully crafted version of reality can make it difficult to discern what is real and what is not, leading to increased skepticism and distrust.

2. The Role of Algorithms in Shaping Trust

One of the most significant ways that social media influences trust is through algorithms that determine what content we see. These algorithms are designed to keep users engaged, but they can also create echo chambers where individuals are only exposed to information that reinforces their existing beliefs. This can deepen divisions and make it harder to trust those with different perspectives.

- **The Challenge of Filter Bubbles**: Algorithms often create "filter bubbles" where users are only shown content that aligns with their preferences, reinforcing existing biases and limiting exposure to diverse viewpoints. This can lead to increased polarization and a breakdown of trust between different communities.
- **Fostering Trust in a Social Media World**: To foster trust in the age of social media, individuals must be conscious of how they engage with content. Critical thinking, fact-checking, and seeking out diverse perspectives are essential for maintaining trust in online interactions.

The Rise of Artificial Intelligence and Trust

Artificial intelligence (AI) is playing an increasingly prominent role in everyday life, from virtual assistants like Siri and Alexa to complex algorithms that shape everything from our online shopping experiences to healthcare decisions. While AI offers incredible potential for improving efficiency and solving problems, it also raises important questions about trust.

1. Trusting AI in Decision-Making

AI is being used in more decision-making processes, from recommending products to diagnosing medical conditions. But can we fully trust machines to make decisions that impact our lives? The opacity of AI algorithms—often referred to as "black box" systems—means that users don't always understand how or why certain decisions are made.

- **The Challenge of Transparency**: Trust in AI systems requires transparency. Users need to understand how AI algorithms work, what data they are using, and how decisions are being made. Without transparency, trust in AI systems is difficult to establish.
- **Building Ethical AI**: For AI to be trusted, it must be developed and deployed with ethical considerations in mind. This includes ensuring that AI systems are free from bias, that they respect user privacy, and that they are designed to benefit society as a whole.

2. The Future of AI and Trust in Human Relationships

As AI continues to evolve, it will play a larger role in human relationships, from virtual therapists and AI-driven dating platforms to robots designed to provide companionship. These developments raise important questions about the future of trust in relationships mediated by technology.

- **AI in Personal Relationships**: AI is increasingly being used in personal relationships, such as through dating apps that use algorithms to match users or virtual therapists that provide mental health support. While these tools can enhance relationships, they also raise concerns about how much we can trust technology to understand and fulfill human emotional needs.
- **The Role of Human Oversight**: As AI becomes more integrated into our lives, maintaining trust will require human oversight and ethical guidelines. Technology should enhance human relationships, not replace them, and should always be designed to prioritize human well-being.

Privacy and Trust in a Digital World

In a world where our personal data is constantly being collected, shared, and sold, privacy has become a central issue when it comes to trust. People are increasingly concerned about how their data is being used, who has access to it, and what protections are in place to safeguard their privacy.

1. The Erosion of Privacy

With the rise of digital platforms, social media, and smart devices, privacy has become a significant concern. People are often unaware of how much personal information is being collected about them, leading to a growing sense of distrust toward tech companies and online platforms.

- **Data Collection and Trust**: Trust in digital platforms hinges on transparency and accountability when it comes to data collection. Companies must be upfront about what data they are collecting, how it is being used, and how it is being protected. Without clear communication, trust in these platforms erodes.
- **Balancing Convenience and Privacy**: Many digital services offer convenience in exchange for personal data. Users must decide how much privacy they are willing to sacrifice for the benefits of these services. Maintaining trust in the digital age requires a balance between convenience and protecting personal privacy.

2. Protecting Privacy to Build Trust

Building trust in a digital world requires stronger privacy protections. Companies that prioritize user privacy and security are more likely to earn the trust of their customers. Additionally, individuals must take an active role in protecting their own privacy by being mindful of the information they share online and using tools to safeguard their data.

- **Data Encryption and Security**: Companies can build trust by implementing strong data encryption and security measures to protect users' personal information. Transparency around security practices is also crucial for maintaining trust.
- **Empowering Users with Control**: Giving users control over their data is another way to build trust. This includes allowing users to manage their privacy settings, opt out of data sharing, and understand how their information is being used.

The Future of Trust in a Hyper-connected World

As technology continues to advance, the future of trust will be shaped by how well we navigate the challenges and opportunities that come with greater connectivity. Trust will need to evolve to meet the demands of a world where interactions are increasingly virtual, data is constantly being exchanged, and AI plays a larger role in decision-making.

1. Building Digital Trust Through Ethical Practices

The future of trust depends on the ethical development and use of technology. Companies, governments, and individuals must work together to create systems that prioritize transparency, privacy, and accountability. Ethical practices will be essential for fostering trust in a digital world.

- **Ethical Tech Development**: As technology continues to evolve, developers and companies must prioritize ethical considerations in the design and implementation of new technologies. This includes addressing issues of bias in AI, ensuring user privacy, and promoting digital equity.
- **Collaborative Governance**: Governments, tech companies, and civil society must collaborate to create frameworks that protect users and promote trust. This includes creating policies around data privacy, AI ethics, and digital security.

2. Embracing Trust in Human Relationships

Despite the increasing role of technology, the foundation of trust remains rooted in human relationships. While technology can facilitate connection, trust will always depend on the authenticity, empathy, and integrity that individuals bring to their interactions with one another.

- **Fostering Authentic Connections**: In a world where digital interactions are commonplace, it's important to prioritize authentic, meaningful connections. Whether online or in person, trust is built through genuine communication, honesty, and vulnerability.
- **Balancing Technology and Human Connection**: As technology continues

to shape our lives, it's essential to strike a balance between digital convenience and human connection. While technology can enhance relationships, trust ultimately comes from the human qualities of compassion, empathy, and integrity.

Conclusion: Trust in the Digital Age

The future of trust in an increasingly digital and interconnected world will be shaped by how we navigate the challenges and opportunities of technology. While the rise of AI, social media, and virtual workspaces presents new complexities, it also offers new avenues for building and sustaining trust. By prioritizing transparency, ethical practices, privacy, and human connection, we can build a future where trust thrives—both in the digital sphere and in our personal relationships.

Trust remains the foundation of all meaningful connections, and while technology will continue to play a larger role in how we interact, the *core elements of trust*—**honesty, integrity, empathy, and accountability**—will always be essential.

13

Conclusion: The Long Journey of Trust

- *Trust as a lifelong practice, not a one-time achievement*
- *How the five trust keys create lasting bonds in all types of relationships*

Final Thoughts

Trust is a lifelong practice that requires ongoing effort, reflection, and commitment. Whether in personal relationships, communities, workplaces, or larger societal systems, trust is built through consistent actions, clear communication, and mutual respect. As the world continues to evolve, so too must our understanding of trust.

By applying the five trust keys—**vulnerability as strength, consistency over time, honest communication, mutual respect,** and **shared accountability**—we can foster deep, lasting connections that endure through change, uncertainty, and growth. *Trust* is not just the glue that holds relationships together; it *is the foundation upon which we build our lives.*

****

Personal Note

Writing **The 5 Trust Keys** has been a deeply personal journey for me. My hope is that the lessons shared here will help you forge stronger, more trusting relationships in every area of your life.

Thank you for joining me on this journey, and I look forward to connecting with you again soon!

Warm regards,
Jordan A. Preston

****

More in the final pages...Keep reading *please* »>

V

Appendix

Let's do some FUN Activities!

14

Trust Exercises for Couples, Families, and Teams

Building and maintaining trust is an ongoing process that requires active engagement. Whether you're working to strengthen trust in a romantic relationship, with family members, or within a team at work, these practical exercises will help you foster deeper connections, improve communication, and create an environment where trust can thrive.

These exercises are designed to be flexible, so they can be adapted to different relationships and contexts. They can be used as one-time activities to address specific trust-building needs or as part of an ongoing practice to nurture trust over time.

1. The Trust Ladder Exercise

Purpose: Build trust by gradually increasing vulnerability and communication in a safe and structured way.

Who It's For: Couples, families, and teams.

Instructions:

The Trust Ladder is a powerful exercise that involves gradually increasing the level of vulnerability and openness in a relationship. The idea is to start with small, low-risk conversations and slowly "climb the ladder" to deeper, more personal topics. This process helps build trust step by step, creating a sense of safety and mutual understanding.

Steps:

1. **Set the Stage**: Sit down together in a quiet, comfortable space where you can speak without distractions. Agree that you will both listen openly and without judgment.
2. **Start with a Low-Risk Question**: Begin with an easy question that doesn't require much vulnerability, such as, "What is something you enjoyed doing this week?" or "What's your favorite movie and why?"
3. **Move Up the Ladder**: Gradually move to more personal or emotionally significant questions. For example, ask, "What's something that has been on your mind lately?" or "What's a challenge you've faced recently, and how did it make you feel?"
4. **Climb to Deeper Levels**: Finally, move into higher-risk, more vulnerable territory by asking questions like, "What is something you're afraid of that you haven't shared with anyone?" or "What's a dream you have that you feel nervous about pursuing?"
5. **Reflect Together**: After completing the exercise, take a moment to reflect on how it felt to share and listen. Talk about what you learned from each other and how the process helped build trust.

2. The 5-Minute Connection Check-In

Purpose: Strengthen trust through daily or weekly check-ins that encourage honest communication.

Who It's For: Couples, families, and teams.

Instructions:

This simple exercise involves setting aside just five minutes each day or week to check in with one another. The focus is on sharing how you're feeling, what's on your mind, and where you may need support. It's a fast, easy way to keep communication open and maintain a foundation of trust.

Steps:

1. **Set Aside Time**: Schedule a time each day or week where you can connect without interruptions—whether it's over breakfast, at the end of the workday, or during a team meeting.
2. **Ask Three Questions**: During your check-in, each person answers these three questions:

- What's one thing that went well for you this week (or today)?
- What's one challenge you faced?
- How can I (or we) support you moving forward?

1. **Listen Without Interruption**: Give each person time to answer the questions without interruption or judgment. This exercise builds trust by encouraging open, honest communication and creating a regular habit of emotional connection.
2. **Reflect**: After the check-in, reflect on what was shared. If anything significant came up, discuss how you can work together to support each other.

3. The "I Appreciate You" Exercise

Purpose: Build trust through expressions of gratitude and appreciation.

Who It's For: Couples, families, and teams.

Instructions:

Appreciation is one of the simplest and most powerful ways to build trust. By acknowledging the positive actions, qualities, or efforts of others, you reinforce their sense of value and strengthen the emotional connection in the relationship. This exercise encourages regular expressions of appreciation, which can prevent feelings of being taken for granted.

Steps:

1. **Schedule Time**: Find a regular time, such as the beginning or end of the week, where everyone in the group (or just you and your partner) can participate. It could be during a family meal, a team meeting, or before

bed.

2. **Share Specific Appreciation**: Each person takes a turn saying, "I appreciate you because..." followed by a specific reason. Focus on the small, everyday things, such as, "I appreciate how you helped me with that project" or "I appreciate how you always make me laugh when I'm feeling down."

3. **Receive the Appreciation**: When someone expresses appreciation toward you, simply say, "Thank you." Avoid deflecting the compliment or minimizing your contribution. Receiving appreciation with gratitude builds trust.

4. **Repeat Regularly**: Make this a regular practice. Over time, the habit of expressing appreciation will create a stronger sense of connection and trust.

4. The Trust Walk

Purpose: Build trust through vulnerability and reliance on another person.

Who It's For: Couples, families, and teams.

Instructions:

The Trust Walk is a classic exercise where one person is blindfolded and guided by another person. This activity requires the "blind" person to trust their guide to lead them safely, while the guide takes responsibility for ensuring their partner's well-being. It's an excellent way to build trust through physical reliance and communication.

Steps:

1. **Set the Scene**: Choose a safe area where you can do the exercise. This could be in a park, your home, or even in a workplace. Ensure there are no obstacles that could cause harm.

2. **Assign Roles**: One person is the "blind" participant, and the other is the guide. The guide is responsible for leading the blindfolded person through the area, giving verbal instructions to keep them safe.

3. **Walk Together**: The guide should lead the blindfolded person by using

calm, clear instructions. For example, they might say, "Take three steps forward" or "Turn to the right and walk two steps." The guide should avoid physical contact unless necessary for safety.

4. **Switch Roles**: Once the first walk is complete, switch roles so both participants experience being both the guide and the blindfolded person.

5. **Reflect**: After the exercise, reflect on how it felt to trust someone else to guide you or to be responsible for another person's safety. Discuss how this experience relates to trust in everyday life.

5. The Conflict Resolution Circle

Purpose: Build trust by resolving conflicts through structured, respectful dialogue.

Who It's For: Couples, families, and teams.

Instructions:

Conflict, when handled poorly, can erode trust in relationships. However, conflict also provides an opportunity to strengthen trust if approached with openness and respect. The Conflict Resolution Circle is an exercise that promotes constructive dialogue in the face of disagreements, helping to resolve issues while maintaining trust.

Steps:

1. **Create a Safe Space**: Gather everyone involved in the conflict and sit in a circle. Ensure that the environment is calm, quiet, and free from distractions.

2. **Set Ground Rules**: Establish ground rules for the conversation, such as:

- Everyone speaks one at a time.
- No interrupting.
- Focus on listening to understand, not just to respond.
- Keep a respectful tone throughout the discussion.

1. **Each Person Shares**: Allow each person to share their perspective on the

conflict without interruption. Encourage them to use "I" statements (e.g., "I feel frustrated when...") rather than placing blame.

2. **Reflect and Acknowledge**: After each person has shared, reflect on what was said. Acknowledge each person's feelings and concerns. This step helps to create a sense of understanding and empathy, which is critical for rebuilding trust.

3. **Work Toward a Solution**: Once everyone has shared and been heard, brainstorm possible solutions together. The goal is to find a resolution that works for everyone, reinforcing the trust that was temporarily damaged by the conflict.

6. The Trust Journal

Purpose: Build self-trust and reflect on moments of trust in your relationships.

Who It's For: Individuals, couples, and families.

Instructions:

The Trust Journal is an individual exercise designed to help you reflect on trust in your relationships and within yourself. By regularly journaling about your experiences with trust, you can identify areas for improvement and celebrate moments where trust was built or strengthened.

Steps:

1. **Choose a Journal**: Select a notebook or journal specifically for this exercise. You can do this daily, weekly, or whenever you feel it's needed.

2. **Reflect on Moments of Trust**: Each time you journal, write about a specific moment when trust was built, maintained, or tested in your relationships. This could be an instance where someone followed through on a promise, where you showed vulnerability, or where you noticed a need for greater trust.

3. **Ask Reflective Questions**: Consider including the following questions in your journal entries:

- What did I do today to build or maintain trust?
- What's one thing I can do to improve trust in my relationships?
- How did I show trust in myself today?

1. **Review Your Progress**: Periodically review your journal entries to see how your understanding of trust has evolved. Reflecting on past experiences can help you gain insights into your relationships and recognize areas where trust has grown.

Final Thoughts on Trust Exercises

Trust is the foundation of all strong relationships, and like any foundation, it must be maintained with care and attention. These exercises are designed to help you actively engage with the process of building, maintaining, and deepening trust in your relationships, whether they are personal, familial, or professional.

The key to successful trust-building is consistency. Make these exercises a regular part of your routine, and remember that trust is something that grows over time through small, meaningful actions. By practicing vulnerability, accountability, honest communication, and empathy, you create an environment where trust can thrive, even in the face of challenges and uncertainty.

You Have the Tools—Now Build the Trust

As you move forward, remember that trust is not built in a day—it's an ongoing journey. Use the tools and exercises in this book to nurture trust in your relationships, and watch as those connections become stronger, deeper, and more resilient. You now have the power to unlock the lasting trust that leads to deep connection and fulfillment in every area of your life.

Thank you for taking this journey of trust. May your relationships be rich with trust, understanding, and love.

Be Blessed!

*** Important Note*** - Support the Author & Make a Difference

Support the Author: Leave a Review!

Thank You for Reading!
If you enjoyed **The 5 Trust Keys**, please consider leaving a review on Amazon. Your feedback helps other readers discover the book! **Simply scan the QR code below to share your thoughts!**
Your review doesn't need to be long or detailed—just a few words about what resonated with you the most would mean the world to me.
I'd love to hear your thoughts!

Your Opinion Matters...

Make a Difference: A Greater Cause!

If **The 5 Trust Keys** has brought you value, has inspired or helped you and/or your relationships, and you'd like to support pending and future work, *I would be deeply grateful for your contribution.* Your support not only:

1. Helps me continue creating **content that matters, and empowers and uplifts others**; but *most importantly,*
2. Also a**ssists with a greater cause**. A portion of all donations will go toward **helping orphans and widows, fighting poverty, and supporting education initiatives** in developing countries.

By giving, you're not only empowering yourself but also transforming the lives of those in need.

How You Can Help?
Please Scan below – Thank you for your generosity!

"Each of you should give what you have decided in your heart to give, not reluctantly or under compulsion, for God loves a cheerful giver." 2 Corinthians 9:7

For God loves a cheerful giver...

www.ingramcontent.com/pod-product-compliance
Lightning Source LLC
Chambersburg PA
CBHW061816250726
48657CB00001B/453